MW00526689

LISTENING TOGETHER

Listening Together

Meditations on Synodality

Timothy Radcliffe

LITURGICAL PRESS
Collegeville, Minnesota

litpress.org

Scripture quotations are from New Revised Standard Version Bible: Catholic Edition © 1989, 1993 National Council of the Churches of Christ in the United States of America. Used by permission. All rights reserved worldwide.

Excerpts from the English translation of *The Roman Missal* © 2010, International Commission on English in the Liturgy Corporation. All rights reserved.

Excerpt from THE POEMS OF EMILY DICKINSON: READING EDITION, edited by Ralph W. Franklin, Cambridge, Mass.: The Belknap Press of Harvard University Press, Copyright © 1998, 1999 by the President and Fellows of Harvard College. Copyright © 1951, 1955 by the President and Fellows of Harvard College. Copyright © renewed 1979, 1983 by the President and Fellows of Harvard College. Copyright © 1914, 1918, 1919, 1924, 1929, 1930, 1932, 1935, 1937, 1942 by Martha Dickinson Bianchi. Copyright © 1952, 1957, 1958, 1963, 1965 by Mary L. Hampson. Used by permission. All rights reserved.

© Libreria Editrice Vaticana-Dicastero per la Comunicazione, 2024
Appendix © 2024 by Timothy Radcliffe
Published in English by Liturgical Press, Collegeville, Minnesota. All rights reserved. No part of this book may be used or reproduced in any manner whatsoever, except brief quotations in reviews, without written permission of Liturgical Press, Saint John's Abbey, PO Box 7500, Collegeville, MN 56321-7500. Printed in the United States of America.

1   2   3   4   5   6   7   8   9

Library of Congress Control Number: 2023952626

ISBN 978-0-8146-8882-3
ISBN 978-0-8146-8883-0 (e-book)

Contents

v

Introduction

All of the chapters of this book were written as small contributions to the 16th Ordinary General Assembly of the Synod of Bishops, which took as its theme "For a Synodal Church: Communion, Participation, and Mission." This gathering came to be known more commonly as the Synod on Synodality. This synodal process began in October 2021 and will conclude in October 2024. So it might be helpful to situate these chapters in this long and complex process, which at this writing has not finished yet.

The title of this synod suggests introversion, the Church turned in on itself. But this is the greatest exercise of listening in the history of humanity. Pope Francis has invited the Church to embark on a radical transformation of our shared life as a Church through listening together to what the Spirit is saying to us and listening to each other. Millions of Catholics have taken part in meetings at parish, diocesan, and continental levels, sharing what they had heard with the organisers of the synod. This is a new way of being Church. We are just at the beginning of discovering how to walk in this way, learning as we go.

The purpose of this consultation was "not to produce documents but to open horizons of hope for the fulfilment of the Church's mission."[1] This hope is not just for the Catholic Church but for all Christians, indeed all of humanity. We seem to be entering a new time of war, violence, and poverty, living under the shadow of the imminent catastrophe of climate change, a world in which the young often struggle to dream of a future.

Out of this long and complex process of consultation came the *Instrumentum Laboris*, or Working Document, which was the basis of the discussions at the first assembly of the Synod on Synodality, which took place in Rome from October 4 to 29, 2023. This was preceded by an ecumenical prayer service, to which the leaders of all the major Christian churches were invited. The members of the synod, including delegates from other churches, were then bussed to the conference centre, the *Fraterna Domus* at Sacrofano, sixteen miles north of Rome, for a

1. XVI General Assembly of the Synod of Bishops, *Instrumentum Laboris for the First Session (October 2023)*, Foreword, n. 3; https://www.synod.va/content/dam/synod/common/phases/universal-stage/il/ENG_INSTRUMENTUM-LABORIS.pdf.

three-day retreat. At the request of Pope Francis, every morning and evening, Mother Maria Ignazia Angelini gave reflections on the scriptural texts of the day, and I offered conferences. These six conferences form the first part of this book.

On October 4, hundreds of members of the synod, including lay people, delegates of other churches, bishops, and cardinals, processed together—a moving image of a shared ecumenical journey—into St. Peter's Square for the formal opening of the synod with a Mass presided over by Pope Francis under a hot sun.

The discussions of the synod were divided into five sections, each beginning with meditations by Mother Maria Ignazia and myself. The three meditations that I gave form the second section of this book.

Following these texts, I have also included a reflection that I prepared after the synod assembly, which I have entitled "Go!" Here I reflect on how far we have come, the challenges we face, and how to prepare for the next session of the synod in October 2024.

The appendix, "Accountability and Co-responsibility in the Government of the Church: The Example of the Dominicans," is based on a paper I gave at a meeting of the Peter and Paul Seminar, which met in Quebec in April 2022, before I knew I would be invited to attend the synod. It was later published in the distinguished periodical for canon law, *Studia Canonica.*[2] My brethren were highly amused that I published an article there, given my almost complete ignorance of canon law!

I thank Mother Maria Ignazia, my fellow spiritual advisor to the synod, for her kindness and encouragement in our shared service. I am indebted to Professors Massimo Faggioli, Anna Rowlands, and Dr. Sarah Parvis for their wise and helpful comments and suggestions for my retreat talks, and to my brother Łukasz Popko, OP, of the Ecole Biblique of Jerusalem, for his inspiring help in listening to the Word of God. "Listen to him!"

2. Timothy Radcliffe, "Accountability and Co-Responsibility in the Government of the Church: The Example of the Dominicans," *Studia Canonica* 56, no. 2 (2022): 587–604.

Retreat Talks

"Hoping against Hope"

October 1, 2023

When the Holy Father asked me to give this retreat, I felt enormously honoured but nervous. I am deeply aware of my personal limitations. I am old—white—a Westerner—and a man! I don't know which is worse! All of these aspects of my identity limit my understanding. So I ask for your forgiveness for the inadequacy of my words.

We are all radically incomplete and need each other. Karl Barth, the great Protestant theologian, wrote of the Catholic "both/and." For example, Scripture *and* Tradition, faith *and* works. He is said to have called it "that damned Catholic 'and' "—"*das verdammte katholische 'Und.*'" So I pray that when we listen to each other during the coming weeks and disagree, we shall often say, "Yes, and . . ." rather than "No!" That is the synodal way. Of course, "no" is also sometimes necessary!

In the second reading at Mass today, St. Paul says to the Philippians: "[M]ake my joy complete: be of the same mind, having the same love, being in full accord and of one mind" (Phil 2:2). We are gathered here because we are *not* united in heart and mind. The vast majority of people who have taken part in the synodal process have been surprised by joy. For many, it is the first time that the Church has invited them to speak of their faith and hope. But some of us are afraid of this journey and of what lies ahead. Some hope that the Church will be dramatically changed, that we shall take radical decisions, for example, about the role of women in the Church. Others are afraid of exactly these same changes and fear that they will only lead to division, even schism. Some of you would prefer not to be here at all. A bishop told me that he prayed *not* to be chosen to come here. His prayer was granted! You may be like the son in today's gospel who at first does not want to go to the vineyard, but he goes!

At crucial moments in the gospels, we always hear these words: "Do not be afraid." St. John tells us, "[P]erfect love casts out fear" (1 John 4:18). So let us begin by praying that the Lord will free our hearts from fear. For some this is the fear of change and for others the fear that nothing will change. But "the only thing we have to fear is fear itself."[1]

1. Franklin D. Roosevelt, First Inaugural Address, March 4, 1933.

Of course, we all have fears, but Aquinas taught us that courage is refusing to be enslaved by fear. May we always be sensitive to the fears of others, especially those with whom we disagree. Like Abraham, we leave not knowing where we are going (see Heb 11:8). But if we free our hearts of fear, it will be wonderful beyond our imagination.

To guide us during this retreat, we shall meditate on the transfiguration. This was the retreat Jesus gave to his closest disciples before they embarked on the *first* synod in the life of the Church, when they walked together (*synhodos*) to Jerusalem. This retreat was needed because they were afraid of the journey they had to make together. Until now they had wandered around the north of Israel. But at Caesarea Philippi, Peter confessed that Jesus was the Christ. Then Jesus invited them to go with him to Jerusalem, where he would suffer, die, and be raised from the dead. They could not accept this. Peter tried to prevent him. Jesus called him "Satan," "enemy." The little community was paralysed. So Jesus took them up the mountain. Let us listen to St. Mark's account of what happened.

> Six days later, Jesus took with him Peter and James and John, and led them up a high mountain apart, by themselves. And he was transfigured before them, and his clothes became dazzling white, such as no one on earth could bleach them. And there appeared to them Elijah with Moses, who

were talking with Jesus. Then Peter said to Jesus, "Rabbi, it is good for us to be here; let us make three dwellings, one for you, one for Moses, and one for Elijah." He did not know what to say, for they were terrified. Then a cloud overshadowed them, and from the cloud there came a voice, "This is my Son, the Beloved; listen to him!" Suddenly when they looked around, they saw no one with them anymore, but only Jesus. (Mark 9:2-8)

This retreat gave them the courage and hope to set off on their journey. It did not always go well. They immediately failed to free the young lad from the evil spirit. They quarrelled about who was the greatest. They misunderstood the Lord. But they were on their way with a fragile hope.

So we, too, prepare for our synod by going on retreat, where, like the disciples, we learn to listen to the Lord. When we set off in three days' time, we shall often be like those disciples and misunderstand each other and even quarrel. But the Lord will lead us onwards toward the death and resurrection of the Church. Let us ask the Lord to give us hope, too: the hope that this synod will lead to a renewal of the Church and not division; the hope that we shall draw closer to each as brothers and sisters. This is our hope not just for the Catholic Church but for all our baptised brothers and sisters. People talk of an "ecumenical winter." We hope for an ecumenical spring.

We also gather in hope for humanity. The future looks grim. Ecological catastrophe threatens the destruction of our home. Wildfires and floods have devoured the world this summer. Small islands are beginning to disappear under the sea. Millions of people are on the road fleeing from poverty and violence. Hundreds have drowned in the Mediterranean, not far from here. Many parents refuse to bring children into a world that appears doomed. In China, young people wear T-shirts saying, "We are the last generation." Let us gather in hope for humanity, especially hope for the young.

I don't know how many parents we have at the synod, but thank you for cherishing our future. After a difficult time in South Sudan, on the frontier with the Congo, I flew back to Britain beside a child who screamed without interruption for eight hours. I am ashamed to confess that I had murderous—Herodian—thoughts! But what more marvellous priestly ministry is there than to raise children and seek to open their minds and hearts to the promise of life. Parents and teachers are ministers of hope.

So we gather in hope for the Church and for humanity. But here is the difficulty: we have contradictory hopes! So how can we hope together? In this we are just like the disciples. The mother of James and John hoped that they would sit on the left and the right of the Lord in glory and so displace Peter; there is rivalry even within the closest circle of Jesus' friends. Judas probably hoped for a rebellion that would throw out the Romans. Some of them probably just hoped not to get killed. But they walk on together. So what *shared* hope can we have at this synod?

At the Last Supper, they received a hope beyond all that they could have imagined: the Body of Christ and his Blood, the new covenant, eternal life. In the light of this eucharistic hope, all their conflicting hopes must have seemed as nothing, except to Judas who despaired. This is what St. Paul called "[h]oping against hope" (Rom 4:18), the hope that transcends all of our hopes.

We, too, are gathered like the disciples at the Last Supper, not as a political debating chamber competing to win. Our hope is eucharistic. I first glimpsed what this means in Rwanda in 1993, when the troubles were just beginning. We had planned to visit our Dominican sisters in the north, but the Belgian ambassador told us we should stay at home. The country was on fire. But I was young and foolish. Now I am old and foolish! That day we saw terrible things: worst, a hospital ward filled with young children who had lost limbs through mines and bombs. One child has lost both legs, an arm and an eye. His father sat beside him weeping. I went into the bush to weep, accompanied by two children each hopping on one leg.

We went to our sisters, but what could I *say*? In the face of such meaningless violence, one has no words. Then I remembered the words of the Lord: "*Do* this in memory of me." We are given something to do. At the Last Supper, there seemed to be no future. All that lay ahead apparently was failure, suffering, and death. And in this darkest moment, Jesus made the most hopeful gesture in the history of the world: "This is my body, given for you. This is my blood, poured out for you." This is the hope that calls us beyond all division. One of the reasons I value going to places of war and suffering is that it is in such places that I learn again and again the beauty of our eucharistic hope.

A priest in the east of Ukraine went to say Mass for some sisters who were moving, faced with the threat of being overwhelmed by the violence of war. Everything was packed. All they could offer for the paten was a red plastic plate. He wrote: "This was how God showed us that he was with us. 'You are sitting in a basement, in the damp and the mould, but I am with you—on a red child's plate, and not on a golden paten.'"[2] This is the eucharistic hope of this synodal journey. The Lord is with us.

The hope of the Eucharist is for what lies beyond our imagination.

> I looked, and there was a great multitude that no
> one could count, from every nation, from all tribes
> and peoples and languages, standing before the

2. Quoted by Jarosław Krawiec, OP, Vicar for Ukraine, in his letter to the Order, Ash Wednesday 2023.

throne and before the Lamb, robed in white, with palm branches in their hands. They cried out in a loud voice, saying,

"Salvation belongs to our God who is seated on the throne, and to the Lamb!" (Rev 7:9-10)

This is the hope that the disciples glimpsed on the mountain in the transfigured Lord. It makes the conflict between our hopes seem minor, almost absurd. If we are truly on the way to the kingdom, does it really matter whether you align yourselves with so-called traditionalists or progressives? Even the differences between Dominicans and Jesuits pall into insignificance! So let us listen to him, come down the mountain, and keep on walking confidently. The greatest gifts will come from those with whom we disagree, if we dare to listen to them.

During our synodal journey, we may worry whether we are achieving anything. The media will probably decide that it was all a waste of time, just words. They will look for whether bold decisions are made on about four or five hot-button topics. But the disciples on that first synod, walking to Jerusalem, did not *appear* to achieve anything. They even tried to prevent blind Bartimaeus from being cured by stopping him near to Jesus. They seemed useless. When the vast hungry crowd gathered around Jesus, the disciples asked the Lord, "How can one feed these people with bread here in the desert?" Jesus asked them what they had—just seven loaves and a few fish (Mark 8:1-10). That was more than enough. If we give generously whatever we have in this synod, that will be more than enough. The Lord of the harvest will provide.

Next to our priory in Baghdad is a home for abandoned children of all faiths, run by Mother Teresa's sisters. I shall never forget little Nura, about eight years old, born without arms or legs, feeding the younger children with a spoon in her mouth. One can wonder what the point of small acts of goodness in a war zone is. Do they make any difference? Aren't they just sticking plasters on a rotting body? We do small good deeds and let the Lord of the harvest give them the fruit he wishes. Today we gather on the feast of St. Thérèse of Lisieux. She was born one hundred fifty years ago. She invites us to follow her "little way" that leads to the kingdom. She said, "Remember that nothing is small in the eyes of God."

In Auschwitz, Primo Levi, the Italian Jew, was given a share of bread every day by an Italian lay man called Lorenzo. He wrote: "I believe that it was really due to Lorenzo that I am alive today; and not so much for his material aid, as for his having constantly reminded me by his presence, by his natural and plain manner of being good, that there still existed a world outside our own, something and someone still pure and whole, not corrupt, not savage . . . something difficult to define, a remote possibility of good, but for which it was worth surviving. Thanks to Lorenzo, I managed not to forget that I myself was a man."[3] The small portion of bread saved his soul.

The last words of St. David, the patron saint of Wales, were "Do simple things well." Our hope is that whatever small deeds we do in this synod will bear fruit beyond our imagination. On that last night, Jesus gave himself to the disciples: "I give myself to you." During this synod let us share not just our words and convictions but ourselves, with eucharistic generosity. If we open our hearts to each other, wonderful things will happen. The disciples gathered all the fragments of bread and fish left over after the feeding of the five thousand. Nothing was lost—as nothing will be lost of every effort we make to reach out to each other.

A final point. Peter tried to stop Jesus from going to Jerusalem because it made no sense to him. It was absurd to go there to be killed. Despair is not pessimism. It is the terror that nothing makes sense anymore. And hope is not optimism but the confidence that all that we live, all our confusion and pain, will somehow be discovered to have meaning. We trust that, as St. Paul says, "Now I know only in part; then I will know fully, even as I have been fully known" (1 Cor 13:12).

---

3. Primo Levi, "The Events of the Summer," in *Survival in Auschwitz* (New York: Touchstone, 1996), 121–22.

Senseless violence destroys all meaning and kills our souls. Meaning is the nourishment of our souls. When St. Oscar Romero, the archbishop of San Salvador, visited the scene of a massacre by the Salvadoran army, he came across the body of a young boy lying in a ditch: "He was just a kid, at the bottom of the ditch, face up. You could see the bullet holes, the bruises left by the blows, the dried blood. His eyes were open, as if asking the reason for his death and not understanding."[4] Yet it was at this moment that he discovered the meaning of his life and the call to give it up. Yes, he was fearful to the end. His dead body was soaked in sweat as he looked at the man who was about to kill him. But he was no longer the slave of fear.

I hope that in this synod there will be no violence! But often we shall probably wonder what the point of it all is. But if we listen to him and listen to each other, we shall come to *understand* the way forward. This is our Christian witness in a world that has often lost confidence that human existence has any meaning. Shakespeare's Macbeth asserts that life is but "a tale told by an idiot, full of sound and fury, signifying nothing."[5] But through our thinking and praying and talking together about

4. Scott Wright, *Oscar Romero and the Communion of the Saints* (New York: Orbis, 2009), 37.

5. *Macbeth*, Act 5, Scene 5.

the great issues that the Church and the world face, we witness to our hope in the Lord who grants meaning to every human life.

Every Christian school is a testimony to our hope in "the light [that] shines in the darkness and the darkness did not overcome it" (John 1:5). In Baghdad the Dominicans founded an academy that has the motto, "Here no questions are forbidden." In the middle of a war zone, a school testifies to our hope that the nonsense of violence will not have the last word. Homs in Syria is a city largely destroyed by senseless violence. But there amid the ruins we discovered a Catholic school. Here the Dutch Jesuit Franz van der Lugt refused to leave despite death threats. He was shot sitting in the garden. But we found an old Egyptian Jesuit who was still teaching. He was training another generation of children to go on trying to make sense of their lives. That is what hope looks like.

So, my brothers and sisters, we may be divided by different hopes. But if we listen to the Lord and to each other, seeking to understand his will for the Church and the world, we shall be united in a hope that transcends our disagreements and be touched by the one whom St. Augustine called that "beauty so ancient and so new. . . . I tasted you and now hunger and thirst for you; you touched me, and I have burned for your peace."[6]

6. *Confessions*, Bk. 7.27, breviary reading for his feast.

In the next session we shall look at another way in which we may be divided: by our understanding of what sort of home the Church is.

At Home in God and God at Home in Us

October 1, 2023

We come to this synod with conflicting hopes. But this need not be an insuperable obstacle. We are united in the hope of the Eucharist, a hope that embraces and transcends all that we long for.

But there is another source of tension. Our understandings of the Church as our home sometimes clash. Every living creature needs a home if it is to flourish. Fish need water and birds need nests. Without a home, we cannot live. Different cultures have different conceptions of home. The *Instrumentum Laboris* tells us that "Asia offered the image of the person who takes off his or her shoes to cross the threshold as a sign of the humility with which we prepare to meet God and our neighbour. Oceania proposed the image of the boat and Africa suggested the image of the Church as the family of God, capable of offering belonging and welcome to all its members in all their variety" (B 1.2). But all of these images show that we need somewhere in which we are both accepted and challenged. At home we are affirmed as we are and invited to be more. Home is where we are known, loved, and safe but challenged to embark on the adventure of faith.

We need to renew the Church as our common home if we are to speak to a world that is suffering from a crisis of homelessness. We are consuming our little planetary home. There are more than 350 million migrants on the move, fleeing war and violence. Thousands die crossing seas to try to find a home. None of us can be entirely at home unless they are. Even in wealthy countries, millions sleep on the street. Young people are often unable to afford a home. Everywhere there is a terrible spiritual homelessness. Acute individualism, the breakdown of the family, ever deeper inequalities, mean that we are afflicted with a tsunami of loneliness. Suicides are rising because without a home, physical and spiritual, one cannot live. To love is to come home to someone.

So what does this scene of the transfiguration teach us about our home, both in the Church and in our dispossessed world? Jesus invited his innermost circle of friends to come apart with him and enjoy this intimate moment. They, too, would be with him in the Garden of Gethsemane. This was the inner circle of those with whom Jesus was most at home. On the mountain he granted them a vision of his glory. Peter wanted to cling to this moment. "Rabbi, it is good for us to be here; let us make three dwellings, one for you, one for Moses, and one for Elijah" (Mark 9:5). He had arrived and wanted this intimate moment to endure.

But they hear the voice of the Father: "Listen to him!" (Mark 9:7). They must come down the mountain and walk to Jerusalem, not knowing what awaited them. They would be dispersed and sent to the ends of the earth to be witnesses to our ultimate home, the kingdom. So here we see two understandings of home: the inner circle at home with Jesus on the mountain and the summons to our ultimate home, the kingdom in which all will belong.

Similarly, different understandings of the Church as home tear us apart today. For some it is defined by its ancient traditions and devotions, its inherited structures and language, the Church we have grown up with and love. It gives us a clear Christian identity. For others, the present Church does not seem to be a safe home. It is experienced as exclusive, marginalizing many people: women, the divorced and remarried. For some it is too Western, too Eurocentric. The *Instrumentum Laboris* also mentions gay people and people in polygamous marriages. They long for a renewed Church in which they will feel fully at home, recognized, affirmed, and safe.

For some the idea of a universal welcome, in which everyone is accepted regardless of who they are, is felt as destructive of the Church's identity. As in a nineteenth-century English song, "If everybody is somebody then nobody is anybody."[1] They believe that identity demands boundaries. But for others, it is the very heart of the Church's identity to *be* open. Pope Francis said, "The Church is called on to be the house of the Father, with doors always wide open . . . where there is a place for everyone, with all their problems and to move towards those who feel the need to take up again their path of faith."[2]

This tension has always been at the heart of our faith, since Abraham left Ur. The Old Testament holds two things in perpetual tension. First the idea of election, being God's chosen people, the people with whom God dwells; this is an identity that is cherished. But also universalism, openness to all the nations, an identity which is yet to be discovered.

Christian identity is both known and unknown, given and to be sought. St. John says, "Beloved, we are God's children now; what we will be has not yet been revealed. What

1. W. S. Gilbert, *The Gondoliers* (1889).

2. Pope Francis, Apostolic Exhortation *Evangelii Gaudium*, November 24, 2013, n. 47, https://www.vatican.va/content/francesco/en/apost
_exhortations/documents/papa-francesco_esortazione-ap_20131124
_evangelii-gaudium.html.

we do know is this: when he is revealed, we will be like him, for we will see him as he is" (1 John 3:2). We know who we are, and yet we do not know who we shall be.

For some of us, the Christian identity is above all given, the Church we know and love. For others Christian identity is always provisional, lying ahead as we journey towards the kingdom in which all walls will fall. Both are necessary! If we stress only our identity as given—*This* is what it means to be Catholic—we risk becoming a sect. If we just stress the adventure towards an identity yet to be discovered, we risk becoming a vague Jesus movement. But the Church is a sign and sacrament of the unity of all humanity in Christ (see *Lumen Gentium* 1) in being both. We dwell on the mountain and taste the glory now. But we walk to Jerusalem, that first synod of the Church.

How are we to live this necessary tension? All theology springs from tension, which bends the bow to shoot the arrow. This tension is at the heart of St. John's Gospel. God makes his home in us: "Those who love me will keep my word, and my Father will love them, and we will come to them and make our home with them" (John 14:23). But Jesus also promises us our home in God: "In my Father's house there are many dwelling places. If it were not so, would I have told you that I go to prepare a place for you?" (John 14:2).

When we think of the Church as home, some of us primarily think of God as coming home to us, and others of us think of coming to home in God. Both are true. We must enlarge the tent of our sympathy to those who think differently. We treasure the inner circle on the mountain, but we come down and walk to Jerusalem, wanderers and homeless. "Listen to him!"

So, first, God makes his home with us. The Word is made flesh in a first-century Palestinian Jew, raised in the customs and traditions of his people. The Word becomes flesh in each of our cultures. In Italian paintings of the annunciation, we see lovely homes of marble, with windows open onto olive trees and gardens of roses and lilies. Dutch and Flemish painters show Mary with a warm oven, well wrapped to keep out the cold. Whatever is your home, God comes to dwell in it. For thirty silent years, God dwelt in Nazareth, an unimportant backwater. Nathanael exclaimed in disgust, "Can anything good come out of Nazareth?" and Philip just replied, "Come and see" (John 1:46).

All of our homes are Nazareth, where God dwells. St. Charles de Foucauld said, "Let Nazareth be your model, in all its simplicity and breadth. . . . The life of Nazareth can be lived anywhere. Live it where is it most useful for your neighbor."[3] Wherever we are and whatever we have done, God comes to stay: "Listen! I am standing at

3. Cathy Wright, LSJ, *Saint Charles de Foucauld: His Life and Spirituality* (Boston: Pauline Books, 2022), 111.

the door, knocking; if you hear my voice and open the door, I will come in to you and eat with you, and you with me" (Rev 3:20).

So we treasure the places where we have met Emmanuel, "God with us." We love the liturgies in which we have glimpsed the divine beauty, the churches of our childhood, the popular devotions. I love the great Benedictine abbey of my school where I first sensed the doors of heaven open. Each of us has our own Mount Tabor, on which we have glimpsed the glory. We need them. So when liturgies are changed or churches demolished, people experience great pain, as if their home in the Church is being destroyed. Like Peter, we wish to stay.

Every local church is a home for God. Our mother Mary appeared in England in Walsingham, the great medieval shrine; in Lourdes; in Guadalupe in Mexico; in Czestochowa in Poland; in La Vang in Vietnam; and Donglu in China. There is no Marian competition. In England we say, "The good news is that God loves you. The bad news is that he loves everyone else as well." St. Augustine said, "God loves each of us as if there were only one of us."[4] In the Basilica of Notre Dame d'Afrique in Algiers, there is inscribed: "*Priez pour nous et pour les Musulmans*"—"Pray for us and for the Muslims."

4. *Confessions*, Bk. 3.

Often priests find the synodal path most difficult to embrace. We clergy tend these places of worship and celebrate its liturgies. Priests need a strong sense of identity, an *esprit de corps*. But who shall we be in this Church that is liberated from clericalism? How can the clergy embrace an identity that is not clerical? This is a great challenge for a renewed Church. Let us embrace it without fear, a new fraternal understanding of ministerial priesthood! Perhaps we can discover how this loss of identity is actually an inherent part of our priestly identity. It is a vocation to be drawn beyond all identities, because "what we will be has not yet been revealed" (1 John 3:2).

God makes his home now in places that the world despises. Our Dominican brother Frei Betto describes how God came to be at home in a prison in Brazil. Some Dominicans were imprisoned for their opposition to the dictatorship (1964–1985). Betto wrote,

> On Christmas day, the Feast of God's homecoming, the joy is overwhelming. Christmas night in prison. . . . Now the whole prison is singing, as if our song alone, happy and free, must sound throughout the world. The women are singing over in their section, and we applaud. . . . Everyone here knows that it's Christmas, that someone is being reborn. And with our song we testify that we too

have been reborn to fight for a world without tears, hatred or oppression. It's quite something to see these young faces pressed against the bars and singing their love. Unforgettable. It's not a sight for our judges, or the public prosecutor, or the police who arrested us. They would find the beauty of this night intolerable. Torturers fear a smile, even a weak one.[5]

So we glimpse the beauty of the Lord in our own Mount Tabor, where, like Peter, we want to pitch our tents. Good! But "listen to him!" We enjoy that moment and then come down the mountain and walk to Jerusalem. We must become, in a sense, homeless. "Foxes have holes, and birds of the air have nests; but the Son of Man has nowhere to lay his head" (Luke 9:58). They walk to Jerusalem, the holy city where God's name dwells. But there Jesus dies outside the walls for the sake of all who live outside the walls, as God revealed himself to his people in the wilderness outside the camp. James Alison wrote, "God is among us as one cast out."[6] "Therefore Jesus also suffered outside the city gate in order to sanctify the people by his own blood. Let us then go to him outside the camp and bear the abuse he endured" (Heb 13:12-13).

5. Frei Betto, aka Carlos Christo, *Letters from a Prisoner of Conscience* (London: Lutterworth, 1978), 127–28.

6. James Alison, *Knowing Jesus* (Springfield, IL: Templegate, 1993), 71.

Archbishop Carlos Azpiroz Costa wrote to the Dominican family when he was Master:

> "Outside the camp" among all those "others" relegated to a place outside the camp, is where we meet God. Itinerancy demands going outside the institution, outside culturally conditioned perceptions and beliefs, because it is "outside the camp" that we meet a God who cannot be controlled. It is "outside the camp" that we meet the Other who is different and discover who we are and what we are to do.[7]

It is in going outside that we reach for a home in which "there is no longer Jew nor Greek, there is no longer slave nor free, there is no longer male nor female; for all of you are one in Christ Jesus" (Gal 3:28).

In the 1980s, reflecting on the Church's response to AIDS, I visited a London hospital. The consultant told me that there was a young man asking for a priest called Timothy. By God's providence I managed to anoint him shortly before he died. He asked to be buried in Westminster Cathedral, the centre of Catholicism in England. At that weekday funeral Mass, he was surrounded by the

7. Fr. Carlos A. Azpiroz Costa, OP, "'Let Us Walk in Joy and Think of Our Savior': Some Views on Dominican Itinerancy" (May 24, 2003), http://dominicains.ca/lettres-des-maitres-de-lordre/?lang=en.

ordinary people who came, as well as by people with AIDS, nurses, doctors, and gay friends. The one who had been on the periphery, because of his illness, because of his sexual orientation, and most of all because he was now dead, was at the centre. He was surrounded by those for whom the Church was home and those who would normally never enter a church.

Our lives are nourished by beloved traditions and devotions. If they are lost, we grieve. But also we must remember all those who do not yet feel at home in the Church: women who feel that they are unrecognised in a patriarchy of old white men like me! People who feel that the Church is too Western, too Latin, too colonial. We must journey towards a Church in which they are no longer at the margin but in the centre.

When Thomas Merton became a Catholic, he discovered "God, that center Who is everywhere, and whose circumference is nowhere, finding me."[8] Renewing the Church, then, is like making bread. One gathers edges of the dough into the centre, and spreads the centre into the margins, filling it all with oxygen. One makes the loaf by overthrowing the distinction between edges and the centre, making God's loaf, whose centre is everywhere and whose circumference is nowhere, finding us.

8. Thomas Merton, *The Seven Storey Mountain: An Autobiography of Faith*, Fiftieth Anniversary Edition (Orlando: Harcourt, 1998), 246.

One last very short word. Time and again during the preparation for this synod, the question was asked: "But how can we be at home in the Church with the horrible scandal of sexual abuse?" For many, this has been the last straw. They have packed their bags and gone. I put this question to a meeting of Catholic head teachers in Australia, where the Church has been horribly disfigured by this scandal. How did they remain? How could they still be at home?

One of them quoted Carlo Carretto (1910–1988), a little brother of Charles de Foucauld. What Carretto said sums up the ambiguity of the Church, my home but not yet my home, revealing and concealing God:

> How much I must criticize you, my Church, and yet how much I love you!
>
> How you have made me suffer and yet how much I owe you.
>
> I should like to see you destroyed and yet I need your presence.
>
> You have given me much scandal and yet you have made me understand holiness. . . .
>
> How often I have felt like slamming the door of my soul in your face—and how often I have prayed that I might die in your sure arms!
>
> No, I cannot be free of you, for I am one with you, even though not completely you.
>
> Then too—where should I go?

To build another?
But I cannot build another without the same
defects, for they are my defects I bear within me.
And again, if I build one, it will be my Church,
and no longer Christ's.[9]

At the end of Matthew's Gospel, Jesus says, "[R]e-member, I am with you always, to the end of the age" (28:20). If the Lord stays, how could we go? God has made himself at home in us with all our scandalous limitations for ever. God remains in our Church, even with all the corruption and abuse. We must therefore remain. But God is with us to lead us out into the wider open spaces of the kingdom. We need the Church, our present home for all its weaknesses, but also to breathe the Spirit-filled oxygen of our future home without boundaries.

9. Carlo Carretto, *I Sought and I Found: My Experience of God and of the Church*, trans. Robert Barr (Maryknoll, NY: Orbis, 1984), 135.

Friendship

October 2, 2023

On the night before he died, Jesus prayed to his Father "that they may be one, as we are one" (John 17:11). But from the beginning, in almost every document of the New Testament, we see the disciples divided, quarrelling, excommunicating each other. We are gathered in this synod because we, too, are divided and hope and pray for unity of heart and mind. This should be our precious witness in a world that is torn apart by violence, conflict, and inequality. The Body of Christ should embody that peace that Jesus promised and for which the world longs.

Yesterday I looked at two sources of division: our conflicting hopes and different visions of the Church as home. But there is no need for these tensions to tear us apart; we are bearers of a hope beyond hope and heirs to the spacious home of the kingdom in which the Lord tells us there are "many dwelling places" (John 14:2).

Of course, not *every* hope or opinion is legitimate. But orthodoxy is spacious and heresy is narrow. The Lord leads his sheep out of the small enclosure of the sheepfold into the wide-open pastures of our faith. At Easter, he will lead them out of the small, locked room into the unbounded vastness of God, "God's plenty."[1]

So let us listen to him together. But how? A German bishop was concerned by "the biting tone" during their synodal discussions. He said they had been "more like a rhetorical exchange of verbal blows" than an orderly debate.[2] Of course, orderly rational debates are necessary. As a Dominican, I could never deny the importance of reason! But more is needed if we are to reach beyond our differences. The sheep trust the voice of the Lord because it is that of a friend. This synod will be fruitful if it leads us into a deeper friendship with the Lord and with each other.

On the night before he died, Jesus addressed the disciples who were about to betray, deny, and desert him, saying, "I have called you friends" (John 15:15). We are

1. Earliest use found in Thomas Becon (1512/13–1567); see *Oxford English Dictionary*, s.v. "God's plenty," at https://www.oed.com/dictionary /gods-plenty_n?tl=true.

2. Christa Pongratz-Lippitt, "Pro-reform German Bishops Warn against Going Too Fast," *The Tablet*, March 20, 2023, https://www.thetablet.co.uk /news/16829/pro-reform-german-bishops-warn-against-going-too-fast.

embraced by the healing friendship of God, which un-
locks the doors of the prisons we create for ourselves.
"The invisible God . . . addresses men and women as his
friends."[3] He opened the way into the eternal friendship
of the Trinity. This friendship was offered to his disciples,
to tax collectors and prostitutes, to lawyers and foreign-
ers. It was the first taste of the kingdom.

Both the Old Testament and classical Greece and
Rome considered such friendships impossible. Friendship was only between the good. Friendship with the
wicked was considered impossible. As Psalm 26 says, "I
hate the company of evildoers, / and will not sit with the
wicked" (v. 5). The bad do not have friends, since they
only collaborate for evil deeds. But our God was always
inclined to make shocking friendships. He loved Jacob
the trickster and David the murderer and adulterer and
Solomon the idolater.

Also, friendship was only possible between equals. But
grace lifts us up into the divine friendship. Aquinas says
"*solus Deus deificat*"—"only God can make us godlike."[4]
Today is the feast of the Guardian Angels, who are signs
of the unique friendship that God has for each of us. The

3. Second Vatican Council, Dogmatic Constitution on Divine Reve-
lation *Dei Verbum* (November 18, 1965), n. 2, in Austin Flannery, ed.,
Vatican Council II: Constitutions, Decrees, Declarations (Collegeville,
MN: Liturgical Press, 1996, 2014), 98.

4. *Summa Theologica* I-II, q. 112, a. 1.

Holy Father said on this feast several years ago, "No one walks alone, and none of us can think he is alone."[5] As we journey, we are each embraced by the divine friendship.

Preaching the Gospel is never just communicating information. It is an act of friendship. A hundred years ago, Vincent McNabb, OP, said, "Love those to whom you preach. If you do not, do not preach. Preach to yourself."[6] St. Dominic was said to have been loved by all since he loved all. St. Catherine of Siena was surrounded by a circle of friends, men and women, lay and religious. They were known as the *Caterinati*, the Catherine people. St. Martin de Porres is often shown with a cat, a dog, and a mouse eating from the same dish. A good image of religious life and also of the synod!

There were no easy friendships between men and women in the Old Testament. The kingdom broke in with Jesus surrounded by his friends, men and women. Even today, many people doubt the possibility of any innocent friendship between men and women. Men fear accusation; women fear male violence; the young fear abuse. We should embody the spacious friendship of God which never harms.

5. Pope Francis, "We All Have an Angel," October 2, 2014, https://www.vatican.va/content/francesco/en/cotidie/2014/documents/papa-francesco-cotidie_20141002_we-all-have-an-angel.html.

6. Vincent McNabb, OP, *An Old Apostle Speaks*, ed. G. Vann (Oxford, 1946), 3.

So we preach the Gospel by friendships that reach across boundaries. God reached across the division between Creator and creature. God's friendship even broke the ultimate barrier, that of death. When Mary Magdalene was walking in the garden, seeking the body of her beloved Lord, she heard a voice, "Mary!" (John 20:16). The Church is the community of friendship that embraces the living and the dead who are alive in God, the communion of saints. They, too, have voices in our synod, which is not just a gathering of those who happen to be alive today.

What impossible friendships can we make? St. Francis befriended the wolf at Gubbio. Are there wolves in the synod with whom you need to make friends?

Friendship reaches across the barriers of religious division. When Blessed Pierre Claverie was ordained the bishop of Oran in Algeria in 1981, he said to his Muslim friends, "I owe to you also what I am today. With you in learning Arabic, I learned above all to speak and understand the language of the heart, the language of brotherly friendship, where races and religions commune with each other. . . . For I believe that this friendship comes from God and leads to God."[7] Notice that friendship made him who he was!

It was for this friendship that he was murdered by terrorists, along with a young Muslim friend, Mohamed

7. Jean Jacques Pérennès, OP, foreword by Timothy Radcliffe, OP, *A Life Poured Out: Pierre Claviere of Algeria* (Maryknoll, NY: Orbis, 2007), viii.

Bouckichi. After his beatification, a play about their friendship, *Pierre et Mohamed*, was performed. Mohamed's mother watched the play about the death of her son and kissed the actor who played him.

The good news the young await to hear from us is that God reaches out to them in friendship. Here is the friendship they desire and for which they search on Instagram and TikTok. I am told the young do not use Facebook now! When I was a teenager, I was befriended by Catholic priests. With them I discovered the joy of faith. Alas, the sexual abuse crisis rendered such friendships suspect. More than a sexual sin, it is a sin against friendship. The deepest circle in Dante's *Inferno* was reserved for those who betray friendship.

So the foundation of all that we shall do in this synod should be the friendships we create. It does not look like much. It will not make headlines in the media. "They came all the way to Rome to make friends! What a waste!" But it is by friendship that we shall make the transition from 'I' to 'we' (see *Instrumentum Laboris* A 1.25). Without it, we shall achieve nothing. When the Anglican Archbishop of Canterbury, Robert Runcie, met St. John Paul II, he was disappointed that no progress towards unity seemed to have been achieved. But the Pope told him to be confident. "Affective collegiality precedes effective collegiality."[8]

8. Cormac Murphy-O'Connor, *An English Spring: Memoirs* (London: Bloomsbury, 2015), 130.

The *Instrumentum Laboris* refers to the loneliness of many priests, and "their need for care, friendship and support" (B 2.4 b). The heart of the priests' vocation is the art of friendship. This is the eternal, equal friendship of our triune God. Then all the poison of clericalism will melt away. The vocation of parenthood can be lonely, too, and needs sustaining friendships.

Friendship is a creative task. In English we say that we *fall* in love, but we *make* friends. Jesus asked the lawyer after the parable of the Good Samaritan, "Which of these three people *made* himself the neighbour of the man who fell into the hands of the robbers?" (Luke 10:36, my translation). He tells the disciples that they must *make* friends by the use of "unrighteous mammon" (Luke 16:9, RSV). In the synod we have the creative task of making improbable friendships, especially with people with whom we disagree. If you think that I am talking nonsense, come and befriend me!

This might sound awful! Imagine me bearing down on you with the grim determination to make you a friend. You will want to run away! But the foundation of friendship is just being with another. It is the enjoyment of another's presence. Jesus invited the inner circle—Peter, James, and John—to be with him on the mountain, as they would be with him in the Garden of Gethsemane. After the ascension, they look for another to replace Judas, someone who has been with the Lord and with them. Peter said he should be "one of the men who have accompanied us during all the time that the Lord Jesus went in and out among us, beginning from the baptism of John until the day when he was taken up from us" (Acts 1:21). Heaven will be just being with the Lord and his friends. Four times during the Eucharist we hear the words, "The Lord be with you." That is the divine friendship. Sister Wendy Beckett described prayer as "being unprotected in the presence of the Lord." Nothing needs to be said. In this retreat we are invited to be silent for much of the time. This silence is not a withdrawal from communication. It is the entry into the deepest communication with those with whom we are walking. It is not the silence of having nothing to say but a taste of the silence shared by those who are close.

In his book on spiritual friendship, St. Aelred of Rievaulx, the twelfth-century Cistercian abbot, wrote, "Here we are, you and I, and I hope that Christ makes a third with us. No one can interrupt us now. . . . So come now, dearest friend, reveal your heart and speak your mind."[9] Will we dare to do speak our minds?

In Dominican general chapters, of course, we debate and take decisions. But we also pray and eat together, go for walks, have a drink, and recreate. We give each other the most precious gift, our time. We build a common

9. Aelred of Rievaulx, *Spiritual Friendship* (Notre Dame, IN: Ave Maria Press, 2008), section 1.1.

life. Then improbable friendships spring up. Ideally, we should do this during these three weeks of the synod, instead of going our separate ways at the end of the day. Let us hope that this will be possible at the next session of this synod.

God's creative love gives us space. Herbert McCabe, OP, wrote, "The power of God is pre-eminently the power to let things be. 'Let there be light'—the creative power is just the power that, because it results in things being what they are, in persons being who they are, cannot interfere with creatures. Obviously creating does not make any difference to things, it lets them be themselves. Creation is simply and solely letting things be, and our love is a faint image of that."[10]

Often no words are needed. A young Algerian woman called Yasmina left a card near the place of Pierre Claverie's martyrdom. She wrote on it, "This evening, Father, I have no words. But I have tears and hope."[11]

If we are with each other in this way, we shall see each other as if for the first time. When Jesus dined with the Pharisee Simon, a woman, possibly the local prostitute, came in and weeping, she washed Jesus' feet with her

10. Herbert McCabe, OP, *God Matters* (London: Darton, Longman and Todd, 1987), 108.

11. Paul Murray, OP, *Scars: Essays, Poems and Meditations on Affliction* (London: Bloomsbury, 2014), 47.

tears. Simon was shocked. Didn't Jesus *see* who she was? But Jesus replied, "Do you see this woman? I entered your house; you gave me no water for my feet, but she has bathed my feet with her tears and dried them with her hair" (Luke 7:44).

Israel had longed to see the face of God. For centuries she had sung, "Let your face shine that we may be saved" (Ps 80:19). But it was impossible to see God and live. Israel longed for what was unbearable, the sight of the face of God. In Jesus, this face was revealed. The shepherds could look on him as a sleeping baby in the manger and live. God's face was seen but it was *God* who died, the eyes closed shut on a cross.

In Eucharistic Prayer II, we pray the dead may be welcomed into the light of God's face. The incarnation is God's visibility. An ancient theologian, possibly St. Augustine, imagines a dialogue with the Good Thief who died with Jesus. He says, "I made no special study of Scripture. I was a full-time robber. But, at a certain moment in my pain and isolation, I found Jesus looking at me and, in his look, I understood everything."[12]

In this time between the first and second coming of Christ, *we* must be that face for each other. We *see* those who are invisible and smile on those who feel ashamed. May the faces of others shine on us when we are ashamed,

12. Quoted by Murray, *Scars*, 143.

too! An American Dominican, Brian Pierce, visited an exhibition of photos of street kids in Lima, Peru. Under the photo of one young kid was the caption, "*Saben que existo pero no me ven*"—"They know that I exist but they do not see me." They know that I exist as a problem, a nuisance, a statistic, but they do not see me!

In South Africa, a common greeting is "*Sawabona*"— "I see you." Millions of people feel invisible. No one looks at them with recognition. Often people are tempted to commit violence just so that people will at least see them! Look, I am here! It feels better to be seen as an enemy than not to be seen at all.

Thomas Merton joined religious life because he wanted to escape the wickedness of the world. But a few years of Cistercian life opened his eyes to the beauty and goodness of people. One day in the street, the scales fell from his eyes. He wrote in his diary, "Then it was as if I suddenly saw the secret beauty of their hearts, the depths of their hearts, where neither sin nor desire nor self-knowledge can reach, the core of their being, the person that each one is in God's eyes. If only they could see themselves as they really *are*. If only we could see each other that way all the time. There would be no more war, no more hatred, no more greed."[13] So formation

13. Thomas Merton, *Conjectures of a Guilty Bystander* (New York: Doubleday/Image, 1989), 156.

for synodality includes learning to see each other, with compassion, the healing gaze.

Our world hungers for friendship, but it is subverted by destructive trends: the rise of populism, in which people are bound together by simplistic narratives, facile slogans, the blindness of the mob. And there is an acute individualism, which means that all I have is *my* story. Terry Eagleton wrote, "Journeys are no longer communal but self-tailored, more like hitchhiking than a coach tour. They are no longer mass products but for the most part embarked on alone. The world has ceased to be story-shaped, which means that you can make your life up as you go along."[14] But "my story" is our story, the Gospel story that can be told in wonderfully different ways.

One last, brief point. C. S. Lewis said that lovers look at each other but friends look in the same direction. They may disagree with each other, but at least they share some of the same questions. " 'Do you *care about* the same truth?' The [one] who agrees with us that some question, little regarded by others, is of great importance, can be our Friend. He need not agree with us about the answer."[15]

---

14. Terry Eagleton, "What's Your Story?," *London Review of Books*, February 16, 2023, https://www.lrb.co.uk/the-paper/v45/n04/terry-eagleton/what-s-your-story.

15. C. S. Lewis, *The Four Loves* (New York: Harcourt, 1988), 66.

The bravest thing we can do in this synod is to be truthful about our convictions but also about our doubts and questions, the questions to which we have no clear answers. Then we shall draw near as fellow searchers, disciples, beggars for the truth. In Graham Greene's *Monsignor Quixote*, a Spanish Catholic priest and a Communist mayor make a holiday together. One day they dare to share their doubts. The priest says, "It is odd how sharing a sense of doubt can bring men together perhaps even more than sharing a faith. The believer will fight another believer over a shade of difference; the doubter fights only with himself."[16]

Pope Francis said in his dialogue with Rabbi Skorka, "The great leaders of the people of God were people who left room for doubt. . . . He who wants to be a leader of the people of God has to give God his space; therefore, to shrink, to recede into oneself with doubt, the interior experiences of darkness, of not knowing what to do; all of that ultimately is very purifying. The bad leader is the one who is self-assured, and stubborn. One of the characteristics of a bad leader is to be excessively normative because of his self-assurance."[17]

16. Graham Greene, *Monsignor Quixote* (New York: Penguin Classics, 1982, 2008), 41.

17. Jorge Mario Bergoglio and Abraham Skorka, *On Heaven and Earth* (New York: Image, 2010, 2013), 52.

If there is no shared concern for the truth, then what basis is there for friendship? Friendship is difficult in our society in part because society has either lost confidence in the truth or else clings to narrow fundamentalist truths that cannot be discussed. Aleksandr Solzhenitsyn said, "One word of truth outweighs the whole world." One of my brethren travelling on a bus overheard two women in the seats in front of him. One was complaining about the sufferings she had to endure. The other one said, "My dear, you have to be philosophical about it." "What does 'philosophical' mean?" "It means you don't think about it."

Friendship flourishes when we dare to share our most profound convictions and our doubts and seek the truth together. What is the point of talking to people who already know everything or who agree completely? But how are we to do so? That is the topic of the conference: the art of conversation.

Conversation on the Way to Emmaus

We are called to walk on the synodal way in friendship. Otherwise we shall get nowhere. Friendship, with God and each other, is rooted in the joy of being together, but we need words, too. At Caesarea Philippi, conversation broke down. Jesus had called Peter "Satan," "enemy." On the mountain Peter still did not know what to say, but the disciples began to listen to Jesus and so the conversation could begin again as they journeyed to Jerusalem.

On the way, the disciples quarrelled, misunderstood Jesus, and eventually deserted him. Silence returned on Good Friday. But the Risen Lord appeared and gave them words of healing to speak to each other. We, too, need healing words that leap across the boundaries that divide us: the ideological boundaries of left and right, the cultural boundaries that divide one continent from another, the tensions that sometimes divide men and women. Shared words are the lifeblood of our Church. We need to find them for the sake of our world in which violence is fuelled by humanity's inability to listen. Words have been weaponised. True conversation leads to conversion. I must confess that much of what I wish to say now comes from a book I have coauthored with a young Polish Dominican, Łukasz Popko, OP, called *Questioning God*.[1]

How should conversations begin? In Genesis, after the Fall, there is a terrible silence. The silent communion of Eden has become the silence of shame. Adam and Eve hide. How can God reach across that chasm? God waits patiently until they have clothed themselves to hide their embarrassment. Now they are ready for the first conversation in the Bible. The silence is broken with a simple question: "Where are you?" (Gen 3:9). It is not a request for information. It is an invitation to step out into the light and stand visibly before the face of God.

Perhaps this is the first question with which we should break the silences that separate us. Not "Why do you hold these ridiculous views on liturgy?" or "Why

1. Timothy Radcliffe and Łukasz Popko, *Questioning God* (London: Bloomsbury, 2023).

are you a heretic or a patriarchal dinosaur?" or "Why are you deaf to me?" But "Where are you?" "What are you worried about?" This is who I am. God invites Adam and Eve to come out of hiding and be seen. If we, too, step out into the light and let ourselves be seen as we are, we shall find words for each other. In the preparation for this synod, often it has been the clergy who have been most reluctant to step out into the light and share their worries and doubts. Maybe we are afraid of being seen to be naked. How can we encourage each other not to fear being seen as we are, weak and sometimes uncertain human beings?

After the resurrection, the silence of the tomb was again broken with questions. In John's Gospel, "Why are you weeping?" (20:13). In Luke, "Why do you look for the living among the dead?" (24:5). When the disciples fled to Emmaus, they were filled with anger and disappointment. The women claimed to have seen the Lord, but they were only women. As today sometimes, women did not seem to count! The disciples were running away from the community of the Church, like so many people today. Jesus did not block their way or condemn them. He asked, "What are you talking about?" (see Luke 24:17). What are the hopes and disappointments that stir in your hearts? The disciples were speaking angrily. The Greek means literally, "What are these words that you are *hurling* at each other?" So Jesus invites them to share their anger.

They had hoped that Jesus would be the one to redeem Israel, but they were wrong. He failed. So, he walked with them and opened himself to their anger and fear.

Our world is filled with anger. We speak of the politics of anger. A recent book is titled *American Rage*. This anger infects our Church, too. A justified anger at the sexual abuse of children. Anger at the position of women in the Church. Anger at those awful conservatives or horrible liberals. Do we, like Jesus, dare to ask each other, "What are you talking about? Why are you angry?" Do we dare to hear the reply? Sometimes I become fed up with listening to all this anger. I cannot bear to hear any more. But listen I must, as Jesus did, walking to Emmaus.

Many people hope that in this synod their voice will be heard. They feel ignored and voiceless. They are right. But we will only have a voice if we first listen. God calls to people by name. Abraham, Moses, Samuel. They each reply with the beautiful Hebrew word *Hinneni*, "Here I am" (see Gen 22:1, Exod 3:4, 1 Sam 3:4). The foundation of our existence is that God addresses each of us by name, and we hear. Not the Cartesian "I think therefore I am," nor "I speak therefore I am," but "I *hear* therefore I am." We are here to listen to the Lord and to each other. As they say, we have two ears but only one mouth! Only after listening comes speech.

We listen not just to what people are saying but to what they are *trying* to say. We listen for the unspoken words, the words for which they search. There is a Sicilian saying: "*La megliu parola è chiddra chi nun si dici*"—"The best word is the one that is not spoken." We listen for how they are right, for their grain of truth, even if what they say is wrong. We listen with hope and not contempt. We had one rule on the General Council of the Dominican Order. What the brethren said was never nonsense. It may be misinformed, illogical, indeed wrong. But somewhere in their mistaken words is a truth I need to hear. We are mendicants after the truth. The earliest brethren said of St. Dominic that he had "humble intelligence of his heart" (*humili cordis intelligentia*).

Perhaps religious orders have something to teach the Church about the art of conversation. St. Benedict teaches us to seek consensus, St. Dominic to love debate, St. Catherine of Siena to delight in conversation, and St. Ignatius of Loyola the art of discernment. St. Philip Neri teaches us the role of laughter, and St. Francis of Assisi teaches us not to take ourselves too seriously!

If we *really* listen, our ready-made answers will evaporate. We will be silenced and lost for words, as Zechariah was before he burst into song. If I do not know how to respond to my sister or brother's pain or puzzlement, I must turn to the Lord and ask for words. Then the conversation can begin.

Conversation needs an imaginative leap into the experience of the other person, to see with their eyes and hear with their ears. We need to get inside their skin. From what experiences do their words spring? What pain or hope do they carry? What journey are they on?

There was a heated debate on preaching in a Dominican general chapter over the nature of preaching, always a hot topic for Dominicans! The document proposed to the chapter understood preaching as dialogical: we proclaim our faith by entering into conversation. But some capitulars strongly disagreed, arguing that this verged on relativism. They said, "We must dare to preach the truth boldly." Slowly it became evident that the quarrelling brethren were speaking out of vastly different experiences.

The document had been written by a brother based in Pakistan, where Christianity necessarily finds itself in constant dialogue with Islam. In Asia there is no preaching without dialogue. The brethren who reacted strongly against the document were mainly from the former Soviet Union. For them, the idea of dialogue with those who had imprisoned them made no sense. To get beyond the disagreement, rational argument was necessary but not enough. You had to *imagine* why the other person held his or her view. What experience led them to this view? What wounds do they bear? What is their joy?

This demanded listening with all of one's imagination. Love is always the triumph of the imagination, as hatred is a failure of the imagination. Hatred is abstract. Love is particular. In Graham Greene's novel *The Power and the Glory*, the hero, a poor, weak priest, says, "When you saw the lines at the corners of the eyes, the shape of the mouth, how the hair grew, it was impossible to hate. Hate was just a failure of imagination."[2]

We need to leap across the boundaries not just of left and right, or cultural boundaries, but generational boundaries, too. I have the happy privilege of living with young Dominicans whose journey of faith is different from mine. Many religious and priests of my generation grew up in strongly Catholic families. The faith deeply penetrated our everyday lives. The adventure of the Second Vatican Council was in reaching out to the secular world. French priests went to work in factories. We took off the habit and immersed ourselves in the world. One angry sister, seeing me wearing my habit, exploded, "Why are you still wearing that old thing?"

Today many young people—especially in the West but increasingly everywhere—grow up in a secular world, agnostic or even atheistic. Their adventure is the discovery of the Gospel, the Church, and the tradition. They joyfully put on the habit. Our journeys are contrary but not contradictory. Like Jesus, I must walk with them and learn what excites their hearts. "What are you talking about?"

2. Graham Greene, *The Power and the Glory* (New York: Penguin, 2003 [1940]), 131.

What films do you watch? What music do you love? Then we shall be given words for each other.

I must imagine how they *see* me! Who am I in their gaze? Once I was cycling around Saigon with a crowd of young Vietnamese Dominican students. This was long before tourists became common. We went around the corner and there were a group of Western tourists. They looked so big and fat and a strange, ugly colour. What odd people. Then I realised that was what I looked like, too!

As the disciples walked to Emmaus, they listened to this stranger who called them fools and contradicted them. He was angry, too! But they began to delight in his words. Their hearts burned within them. During the synod, can we learn the ecstatic pleasure of disagreement leading to insight? Hugo Rahner, Karl's younger brother (and much easier to understand!), wrote a book on *homo ludens*, playful humanity.[3] Let us learn to speak to each other playfully, as Jesus and the Samaritan woman at the well do in John 4!

In today's first reading at Mass, we shall hear that in the fullness of time, "the city shall be full of boys and girls playing in its streets" (Zech 8:5). The gospel invites us *all* to become children: "Truly I tell you, unless you

3. Hugo Rahner, SJ, *Man at Play, or Did You Ever Practice Eutrapelia?*, trans. Brian Battershaw and Edward Quinn (London: Compass Books, 1965).

change and become like children, you will never enter the kingdom of heaven" (Matt 18:3). We prepare for the kingdom by becoming playful, childlike but not childish. Sometimes we in the Church are afflicted by a dull, joyless seriousness. No wonder people are bored! Can there be preaching without laughter?

On the night of the new millennium, while I was waiting in Cote d'Ivoire to catch a flight to Angola, I sat in the dark with our Dominican students, sharing a beer and talking easily about what was dearest to us. We delighted in the pleasure of being different, of having different imaginations. The delight in difference! I feared I would miss the plane, but it was three days late! Difference is fertile, generative. Each of us is the fruit of the wonderful difference between men and women. If we flee from difference, we shall be barren and childless, in our homes and our Church. Again, we thank all the parents in this synod! Families can teach the Church a lot about how to cope with difference. Parents learn how to reach out to children who make incomprehensible choices and yet know they still have a home.

If we can discover the pleasure of imagining why our sisters and brothers hold the views we find odd, then a new springtime will begin in the Church. The Holy Spirit will give us the gift of speaking other languages.

Notice that Jesus did not attempt to control the conversation. He asked what *they* were talking about. He went where *they* went, not where he wished to go. He accepted *their* hospitality. A real conversation cannot be controlled. One surrenders oneself to its direction. We cannot anticipate where it will take us, to Emmaus or Jerusalem. Where will this synod lead the Church? If we knew in advance, there would be no point in having it! Let us be surprised!

True conversation is therefore risky. If we open ourselves to others in free conversation, we shall be changed. Each profound friendship brings into existence a dimension of my life and identity that has never existed before. I become someone I have never quite been before. I grew up in a wonderful, conservative Catholic family. When I became a Dominican, I became friends with people of different backgrounds, utterly different politics, which my family found disturbing! Who, then, was I when I went home to stay with my family? How did I reconcile the person who I was with them and the person that I was becoming with the Dominicans? I did not know. I am still discovering.

Every year I get to know newly joined Dominicans with different convictions and different ways of seeing the world. If I open myself to them in friendship, who will I become? Even at my advanced age, my identity must remain open. In Madeleine Thien's novel about Chinese immigrants in the USA, *Do Not Say We Have Nothing*, one of the characters says, "Don't ever try to be only a single thing, an unbroken human being. If so many people love you, can you honestly be one thing?"[4] If we open ourselves to multiple friendships, we shall not have a neat, tightly defined identity. If we open ourselves to each other in this synod, we shall all be changed. It will be a little death and resurrection.

A Filipino Dominican novice master had a notice on his door: "Forgive me. I am a work in progress." Coherence lies ahead, in the kingdom. Then the wolf and the lamb *within* each of us shall be at peace with each other. If we have closed, fixed identities written in stone now, we shall never know the adventure of new friendships that will unfold new dimensions of who we are. We shall not be open to the spacious friendship of the Lord.

When they reached Emmaus, the flight from Jerusalem stopped. Jesus looked as if he wished to go further, but with glorious irony they invited the Lord of the Sabbath to rest with them. "Stay with us, because it is almost evening and the day is now nearly over" (Luke 24:29). Jesus accepted their hospitality as the three strangers in Genesis 18 accepted the hospitality of Abraham. God is our guest. We, too, must have the humility to be guests. The German submission to the General Secretariat of the Synod said that we must leave "the comfortable position

4. Madeleine Thien, *Do Not Say We Have Nothing* (London: Granta, 2016), 457.

of those who give hospitality to allow ourselves to be welcomed into the existence of those who are our companions on the journey of humanity."[5]

Marie-Dominique Chenu, OP, the grandfather of the Second Vatican Council, went out most evenings, even when he was eighty. He went out to listen to trade union leaders, academics, artists, families, and to accept their hospitality. Late in the evening, we would meet for a beer and he would ask, "What did you learn today? At whose table did you sit? What gifts did you receive?" The Church in every continent has gifts for the universal Church. To take just one example, my brethren in Latin America, especially our beloved brother Gustavo Gutiérrez, taught me to open my ears to the words of the poor. Shall we hear them in our debates this month? What shall we learn from our brothers and sisters in Asia and Africa?

"When he was at the table with them, he took bread, blessed and broke it, and gave it to them. Then their eyes were opened, and they recognized him; and he vanished from their sight" (Luke 24:30-31). Their eyes were opened. The previous time that we heard that phrase in

5. General Secretariat of the Synod, *"Enlarge the Space of Your Tent" (Is 54:2)*, Working Document for the Continental Stage, Vatican City, October 2022, n. 3.31, https://www.synod.va/content/dam/synod/common/phases /continental-stage/dcs/Documento-Tappa-Continentale-EN.pdf.

Scripture was when Adam and Eve took the fruit from the tree of life and "then the eyes of both were opened, and they knew that they were naked" (Gen 3:7). This is why some ancient commentators understood the disciples on the road to Emmaus to be Cleopas and his wife, a married couple, a new Adam and Eve. Now they ate the bread of life.

One last small thought. When Jesus vanished from their sight, they said, "Were not our hearts burning within us while he was talking to us on the road?" (Luke 24:32). It is as if it was only *afterwards* that they become aware of the joy they had as walked with the Lord. St. John Henry Newman said that it is only as we look backwards at our lives that we become aware of how God was always with us. I pray that this will be our experience, too.

During this synod, we shall be like these disciples. Sometimes we shall not be aware of the Lord's grace working in us and may even think that it is all a waste of time. But I pray God that afterwards, looking backwards, we shall become aware that God was with us all the time and that our hearts burnt within us.

Authority

October 3, 2023

Now we come to a topic that is key to our understanding of the synodal path: authority. If we understand authority in political terms, an executive authority, then the synod will result in disappointment and anger.

There can be no fruitful conversation between us unless we recognise that each of us speaks with authority. We all are baptised into Christ: priest, prophet, and king. The International Theological Commission, writing on the *sensus fidei*,[1] quotes St. John: "[Y]ou have been anointed by the Holy One, and all of you have

1. International Theological Commission, Sensus Fidei *in the Life of the Church* (Vatican, 2014), https://www.vatican.va/roman_curia

knowledge. . . . [T]he anointing that you received from [Christ] abides in you, and so you do not need anyone to teach you. . . . [H]is anointing teaches you about all things" (1 John 2:20, 27).

Many lay people have been astonished during the preparation of this synod to find that they are listened to for the first time. They had doubted their own authority and asked, "Can I really offer something?" (B 2.53). But it is not just the laity who lack authority. The whole Church is afflicted by a crisis of authority. An Asian archbishop complained to me that he had no authority. He said, "The priests are all independent barons, who take no notice of me." Many priests, too, say they have lost all authority. The sexual abuse crisis has discredited us.

Our whole world is suffering a crisis of authority. All institutions have lost authority. Politicians, the law, the press have all felt authority draining away. Authority always seems to belong to other people: dictators who are coming into power in many places, the new media, celebrities and influencers. The world hungers for voices that will speak with authority about the meaning of our lives. Dangerous voices threaten to fill the vacuum. It is a world powered not by authority but by contracts—even in the family, the university, and the Church.

/congregations/cfaith/cti_documents/rc_cti_20140610_sensus-fidei _en.html.

So how may the Church recover authority and speak to our world, which hungers for voices that ring true? Luke tells us that when Jesus taught, "[t]hey were astounded at his teaching, because he spoke with authority" (Luke 4:32). He commanded the demons and they obeyed. Even the wind and sea obeyed him. He even had the authority to summon his dead friend to life: "Lazarus, come out!" (John 11:43). Almost the final words of Matthew's Gospel are "All authority in heaven and on earth has been given to me" (28:18).

But halfway through the Synoptic Gospels, at Caesarea Philippi, there is a massive crisis of authority, which makes our contemporary crisis look like nothing. Jesus told his closest friends that he had to go to Jerusalem where he would suffer, die, and rise again. They did not accept his word. So Jesus took them up the mountain and was transfigured in their sight.

His authority was revealed through the prism of his glory and the witness of Moses and Elijah. It was an authority that touched their ears and their eyes, their hearts and their minds. Their imagination! Now at last, they listen to him!

Now they have both fear and joy. "It is good for us to be here." As Teilhard de Chardin famously said, "Joy is the infallible sign of the presence of God." This is the joy that Mother Maria Ignazia talked about this morning, Mary's joy. Without joy, none of us has any authority at all. No

one believes a miserable Christian! In the transfiguration, this joy flows from three sources: beauty, goodness,
and truth. We could mention other forms of authority.
In the *Instrumentum Laboris*, the authority of the poor
is stressed. There is the authority of the tradition and of
the hierarchy with its ministry of unity. I think a bishop
will speak of this later in the synod.

I suggest that authority is multiple and mutually en-
hancing. There need be no competition, as if the laity
can only have more authority if the bishops have less,
or that so-called conservatives compete for authority
with progressives. We might be tempted to call down
fire on those we see as opposed to us, like the disciples
in today's gospel (Luke 9:51-56). But in the Trinity, there
is no rivalry. The Father and the Son and the Holy Spirit
do not compete for power, just as there is no competition
between our four Gospels.

We shall speak with authority to our lost world if in
this synod we transcend competitive ways of existing
and talking. Then the world will recognise the voice of
the shepherd who summons us to life. Let us look at this
scene on the mountain and see the interaction of different forms of authority.

Beauty

First there is beauty or glory. The two are virtually synony-
mous in Hebrew. Bishop Robert Barron said somewhere

—and forgive me Bishop Bob, if I am misquoting you— that beauty can reach people who reject other forms of authority. A moral vision can be perceived as moralistic: "How dare you tell me how to live my life?" The authority of doctrine may be rejected as oppressive: "How dare you tell me what to think?" But beauty has an authority that touches our intimate freedom, which is why for many it first opens the door to faith.

Beauty opens our imagination to the transcendent, the homeland for which we long. The Jesuit poet Gerard Manley Hopkins calls God "beauty's self and beauty's giver."[2] Aquinas says that it reveals the final end of our lives, like the target at which the archer aims.[3]

No wonder that Peter did not know what to say. Beauty carries us beyond words. It has been claimed that every adolescent has some experience of transcendent beauty. If they do not have guides, as the disciples had Moses and Elijah, the moment passes. When I was a sixteen-year-old boy at a Benedictine school, I had such a moment in the great abbey church, and I had wise monks to help me understand.

But not all beauty speaks of God. Nazi leaders loved classical music. On the feast day of the Transfiguration, an atomic bomb was dropped on Hiroshima in a hideous

2. Gerard Manley Hopkins, "The Leaden Echo and the Golden Echo" (1918).

3. *Summa Theologica* III, q. 45, a. 1.

parody of the divine light. Beauty can deceive and seduce. Jesus said, "Woe to you, scribes and Pharisees, hypocrites! For you are like whitewashed tombs, which on the outside look beautiful, but inside they are full of the bones of the dead and of all kinds of filth" (Matt 23:27).

But the divine beauty on the mountain shined most brightly outside the holy city, when the glory of the Lord was revealed on the cross. God's beauty is disclosed most radiantly in what seems most ugly. One must go to the places of suffering to glimpse the beauty of God.

I visited Kinshasa, the capital of the Democratic Republic of the Congo, during a time of civil war and upheaval. The city was almost surrounded by armies. The frontiers were closed, and I could not find a plane to return me to Rome for a meeting of the General Council. When I went to Mass, already in the sacristy, the singing and dancing had begun. It was infectious. It was a light shining in the darkness that the darkness could not overcome, as St. John says. Maybe we need our African brothers and sisters to teach us how to sing and dance. Then people would be drawn to our faith.

Etty Hillesum, the Jewish mystic drawn to Christianity, found it even in Auschwitz: "I want to be there in the thick of what people call 'horror' and still be able to say 'Life is beautiful.' "[4] Every renewal of the Church has

4. Etty Hillesum, *An Interrupted Life: The Diaries and Letters of Etty Hillesum 1941–43* (London: Persephone Books, 2007), 276.

gone with an aesthetic revival: Orthodox iconography, Gregorian chant, Counter-Reformation baroque (not my favourite!), nineteenth-century Methodist hymns. The Reformation was, in a sense, a parting of ways of aesthetic visions. What aesthetic renewal do we need today to open a glimpse of transcendence, especially in places of desolation and suffering? How can we disclose the beauty of the cross?

I love the abstract paintings of the Dominican artist Kim En Joong. He gave me one for my office. When I proudly showed it to my mother, she looked at it sceptically and said, "It looks like your habit after a messy breakfast!"

When the Dominicans first arrived in Guatemala in the sixteenth century, beauty opened the way for them to share the Gospel with the indigenous people. They refused the protection of the Spanish conquistadors. The friars taught the local indigenous merchants Christian songs, to be sung as they travelled in the mountains selling their goods. This beauty opened the way for the brethren who could then ascend safely into the region still known as *Vera Paz*, True Peace. But eventually the soldiers came and killed not just the indigenous people but our brethren who tried to protect them.

What songs can enter the new continent of the young? Who are our musicians and poets? So beauty opens the imagination to the ineffable end of the journey. But we may be tempted, like Peter, to stay there. Other sorts of imaginative engagement are necessary to bring us down the mountain for the first synod on the way to Jerusalem. The disciples are offered two interpreters of what they see, Moses and Elijah, the Law and the Prophets. Or goodness and truth.

Goodness

Moses led Israel out of slavery into freedom. The Israelites did not wish to go. They hungered for the safety of Egypt. They feared the freedom of the desert, just as the disciples feared to make the journey to Jerusalem. In *The Brothers Karamazov* by Dostoevsky, the Grand Inquisitor asserts that "nothing has ever been more insupportable for . . . human society than freedom. . . . In the end they will lay their freedom at our feet, and say to us, 'Make us your slaves, but feed us.'"[5] But Moses, to whom God spoke as to a friend (see Exod 33:11), summons us to find our freedom in God even when we must pass through the desert.

The saints have the authority of courage. They dare us to take to the road. They invite us come with them on the risky adventure of holiness. St. Teresa Benedicta of the Cross was born into an observant Jewish family but

5. Fyodor Dostoevsky, *The Brothers Karamazov*, trans. Constance Garnett (London: Heinemann, 1912), 266–67.

became an atheist when she was a teenager. But when by chance she picked up St. Teresa of Avila's autobiography, she read it all night. She said, "When I had finished the book, I said to myself: 'This is the truth.'" This led her to death in Auschwitz. That is the authority of holiness. It invites us to let go of control of our lives and let God be God.

The most popular book of the twentieth century was *The Lord of the Rings* by J. R. R. Tolkien. It is a deeply Catholic novel. He claimed it was the romance of the Eucharist, the adventure of faith. The martyrs were the earliest authorities in the Church, because boldly they gave everything. G. K. Chesterton said, "Courage is almost a contradiction in terms. It means a strong desire to live taking the form of readiness to die."[6] Are we afraid to present the dangerous challenge of our faith? Herbert McCabe, OP, said, "If you love, you will be hurt, perhaps killed. If you do not love, you are dead already." Young people are not attracted to our faith if we domesticate it, but they may be excited if we are unafraid to present it as the risky embrace of life.

"[P]erfect love casts out fear" (1 John 4:18). Brother Michael Anthony Perry, the former minister general of the Franciscans, said: "In baptism, we have renounced

6. G. K. Chesterton, *Orthodoxy* (London: Hodder and Stoughton, 1996), 134.

the right to have fear."[7] I would say we have renounced the right to be *enslaved* by fear. The courageous know fear. We shall only have authority in our fearful world if we are seen to risk everything. When our European brothers and sisters went to preach the Gospel in Asia four hundred years ago, half of them died before they arrived, of disease, shipwreck, piracy. Would we have their mad courage?

Henri Burin de Roziers (1930–2017) was a French Dominican lawyer based in the Brazilian Amazon. He took to court the great landowners who often enslave the poor, forcing them to work on their vast estates and killing them if they tried to escape. Henri received innumerable death threats. He was offered police protection, but he knew that they would most likely be the ones to kill him. When I stayed with him, he offered me his room for the night. The next day he told me that he could not sleep in case they came for him and got me by mistake!

So the authority of beauty speaks of the end of the journey, the homeland we have never seen. The authority of holiness speaks of the journey to be made if we are to arrive there. It is the authority of those who give their lives away. The Irish poet Pádraig Pearse proclaimed:

7. Riccardo Benotti, *Viaggio nella vita Religiosa: interviste e incontri* (Vatican City: Libreria Editrice Vaticana, 2016), 66.

I have squandered the splendid years that the Lord
  God gave to my youth
In attempting impossible things, deeming them
  alone worth the toil. . . .
Lord, if I had the years I would squander them
  over again,
Aye, fling them from me![8]

Truth

Then there is Elijah. The prophets are the truth-tellers.
Elijah saw through the fantasies of the prophets of Ba'al
and heard the still, small voice of silence on the mountain. *Veritas*, Truth, the motto of the Dominican Order.
It drew me to the Dominicans even before I met one,
which was perhaps providential!

Our world has fallen out of love with the truth—fake
news, wild assertions on the internet, mad conspiracy
theories. Yet buried in humanity is an ineradicable instinct for the truth, and when it is spoken, it has some
last vestiges of authority. The *Instrumentum Laboris* is
unafraid to be truthful about the challenges we must
address. It speaks openly about the hopes and sorrows,
the anger and the joy of the people of God. How can we

8. Pádraig Pearse, "The Fool" (1915).

draw people to the One who is the Truth if we are not truthful about ourselves?

Let me mention just two ways in which this prophetic tradition of truth-telling is urgently needed today. First of all, in speaking truthfully of the joys and sufferings of the world. In Hispaniola, Bartolome de Las Casas had been leading a life of mediocrity when he read the sermon preached by Antonio de Montesinos, OP, in the Advent of 1511, confronting the conquistadors about their enslavement of the indigenous people: "Tell me, by what right or by what interpretation of justice do you keep these Indians in such a cruel and horrible servitude? By what authority have you waged such detestable wars against people who were once living so quietly and peacefully in their own land?"[9] Las Casas read this, knew it was true, and repented. So in this synod, we shall listen to people who will speak truthfully about "[t]he joys and hopes, the grief and anguish of the people of our time."[10]

9. As recorded in Bartolomé de Las Casas, *Historia de Las Indias in Obras escogidas, estudio critic y edicion* by Juan Perez de Tudela Buesco, 5 vols. (Madrid: Atlas, 1957–58), vol. 2, col. 176. This translation is by Roger Ruston, *Human Rights and the Image of God* (London: SCM Press, 2004), 66.

10. Second Vatican Council, Pastoral Constitution on the Church in the Modern World *Gaudium et Spes* (December 7, 1965), n. 1, in Flannery, *Vatican Council II*, 163.

For truth, we also need disciplined scholarship that resists our temptation to use the word of God and the teachings of the Church for our own purposes. "God must be right because he agrees with me!" Biblical scholars, for example, bring us back to the original texts in their foreignness, their otherness. When I was in hospital, a nurse said to me that he wished that he knew Latin so that he could read the Bible in the original language. I said nothing! True scholars oppose any simplistic attempt to enlist the Scriptures or tradition for our personal campaigns. God's word belongs to God. Listen to him. We do not own the truth. The truth owns us.

All love opens us to the truth of the other person. We discover how they remain, in a sense, unknowable. We cannot take possession of them and use them for our purposes. We love them in their otherness, in their uncontrollable freedom.

So on the mountain of the transfiguration, we see how different forms of authority are invoked to lead the disciples beyond that great crisis of authority of Caesarea Philippi. All of these and others are necessary. Without truth, beauty can be vacuous. As someone said, "Beauty is to truth as deliciousness is to food." Without goodness, beauty can deceive. Goodness without truth collapses into sentimentality. Truth without goodness leads to the Inquisition. St. John Henry Newman spoke beautifully of the multiple forms of authority, of governance, reason, and experience.

We all have authority, but differently. Newman wrote that if the authority of government becomes absolute, it will be tyrannical. If reason becomes the sole authority, we fall into arid rationalism. If religious experience is the only authority, then superstition will win. A synod is like an orchestra, with different instruments having their own music. This is why the Jesuit tradition of discernment is so fruitful. Truth is not arrived at by majority vote, any more than an orchestra or a football team are led by voting!

The authority of leadership is surely ensuring that the conversation of the Church is fruitful, that no one voice dominates and drowns out others. It discerns the hidden harmony. The hierarchy, with its ministry of unity, ensures that the conversation chimes with that of the whole Church, across space and time. The councils of the past have a voice in our conversations that cannot be denied.

Jonathan Sacks, chief rabbi of Great Britain, wrote, "In turbulent times, there is an almost overwhelming temptation for religious leaders to be confrontational. Not only must truth be proclaimed but falsehood must be denounced. Choices must be set out as stark divisions. Not to condemn is to condone." But, he asserts, "a prophet hears not one imperative but two: guidance and compassion, a love of truth and an abiding solidarity with those for whom that truth has become eclipsed. To preserve tradition and at the same time defend those others condemn is the difficult, necessary task of religious leadership in an unreligious age."[11]

All power comes from our triune God, the one in whom all is shared. The Italian theologian Leonardo Paris asserts, "The Father shares his power. With everyone. And he configures all power as shared. . . . It is no longer possible to quote Paul—'There is no longer Jew or Greek; there is no longer slave or free; there is no longer male and female; for all of you are one in Christ Jesus' (Gal 3:28)—and appeal to synodality without recognising that this means finding concrete historical forms so that each one is recognised as having the power that the Father has willed to entrust to him or her."[12]

If the Church becomes truly a community of mutual empowerment, we shall speak with the authority of the Lord. Becoming such a Church will be painful and beautiful. This is what we shall look at in the last conference.

11. Jonathan Sacks, "Elijah and the Still, Small Voice," rabbisacks.org/covenant-conversation/pinchas/elijah-and-the-still-small-voice.

12. Leonardo Paris, *L'erede: Una cristologia* (Breschia: Queriniana, 2021), 220–21.

The Spirit of Truth

October 3, 2023

The disciples see the glory of the Lord and the witness of Moses and Elijah. Now they dare to come down the mountain and walk to Jerusalem. In today's gospel (Luke 9:51-56), we see them on the way. They encounter the Samaritans who oppose them because they are going to Jerusalem. The immediate reaction of the disciples is to call down fire from heaven and destroy them. Well, they have just seen Elijah, and this is what he did to the prophets of Ba'al! But the Lord rebukes them. They still have not understood the journey beyond violence on which the Lord is leading them.

During the next three weeks, we may be tempted to call down fire from heaven on those with whom we disagree! Perhaps on me! Our society is filled with burning rage. The Lord summons us to banish such destructive urges from our meeting.

This pervasive rage springs from fear, but we need not be afraid. The Lord has promised the Holy Spirit who will guide us into all truth. On the night before he died, Jesus said, "I still have many things to say to you, but you cannot bear them now. When the Spirit of truth comes, he will guide you into all the truth; for he will not speak on his own, but will speak whatever he hears, and he will declare to you the things that are to come" (John 16:12-13).

Whatever conflicts we have on the way, we are sure of this: the Spirit of truth is leading us into all truth. But this will not be easy. Jesus warns the disciples: "I still have many things to say to you, but you cannot bear them now." At Caesarea Philippi, Peter could not bear to hear that Jesus would have to suffer and die. On this last evening before the death of Jesus, he could not bear the truth that he would deny Jesus. Being led into the truth means hearing things that are unpalatable, difficult to hear.

What are the truths that we find hard to face today? It has been deeply painful to face the extent of sexual abuse and corruption in the Church. It has seemed like a nightmare from which one hopes to awake. But if we dare to face this shameful truth, the truth will set us free. Jesus promises that "you will have pain, but your pain will turn into joy" (John 16:20), as in the labour pains of a woman giving birth. These days of the synod will sometimes be painful, but if we let ourselves be guided by the Spirit, these will be the birth pangs of a reborn Church.

This is our witness to a society that also flees from the truth. The poet T. S. Eliot wrote that "human kind / Cannot bear very much reality."[1] We are careering towards an ecological catastrophe, but our political leaders mostly pretend that nothing is happening. Our world is crucified by poverty and violence, but the wealthy countries do not want to see the millions of our brothers and sisters who suffer and look for a home.

Western society is afraid to face the truth that we are vulnerable mortal beings, flesh and blood men and women. We flee the truth of our bodily existence, pretending that we can just self-identify as we wish, as if we were just minds. Cancellation culture means that people with whom we disagree must be silenced, deplatformed, just as the disciples wished to call down fire on the Samaritans who did not welcome Jesus. What are the painful truths that our brothers and sisters from other continents fear to face? It is not for me to say.

If we dare to be truthful about who we are—mortal, vulnerable human beings and brothers and sisters in a Church that has always been heroic *and* corrupt—we

1. T. S. Eliot, "Burnt Norton," in *Four Quartets* (1936).

shall speak with authority to a world that still hungers for truth even when it fears it is unattainable. This requires courage, which for Aquinas was *fortitudo mentiis*, the strength of mind to see things as they are, to live in the real world. The American poet Maya Angelou said, "Courage is the most important of the virtues, because without it, no other virtue can be practiced consistently."[2]

Once when St. Oscar Romero was returning home to El Salvador, an immigration official said, "There goes the truth." He was truthful in the face of death. Sitting on a bench, he asked a friend if he was afraid to die. The friend said he was not. Romero replied, "But I am. I am afraid to die." It was this truthfulness that made his martyrdom so beautiful. Ever since he had looked at the mutilated body of his Jesuit friend Rutilio, he had known what awaited him, but he did not flee his destiny.

On that last night, Jesus warned his disciples that if they belonged to him, the true vine, they would be pruned, so that they may bear more fruit (see John 15:1-2). In this synod, we may feel we are being pruned! It is so that we may bear more fruit. This may mean that we are pruned of illusions and prejudices that we have about

2. Maya Angelou, in Anne Ju, "Courage Is the Most Important Virtue, Says Writer and Civil Rights Activist Maya Angelou at Convocation," *Cornell Chronicle*, May 24, 2008.

each other, pruned of our fears and narrow ideologies, pruned of our arrogance and self-importance.

One of my young brethren encouraged me to speak personally at this point, though I hesitate to do so. A couple of years ago I had a massive operation for cancer of the jaw. It took seventeen hours. I was in hospital for five weeks, unable to eat or drink. Often confused as to where I was and who I was, I was stripped of dignity and completely dependent on other people for even the most basic needs. It was a terrible pruning. It was also a blessing. In this moment of helplessness, I could make no claims to importance, claim no achievements. I was just another ill person in a bed in the ward, with nothing to give. I could not even pray much. Then my eyes were opened a bit more to the utterly gratuitous, unmerited love of the Lord. I could do nothing to deserve it, and it was marvellous that I did not have to do so.

The Spirit is in each of us, leading us together into all truth. I was ordained by the great Bishop Butler, the only person in the Second Vatican Council who spoke perfect Ciceronian Latin! He loved to say, "*Ne timeamus quod veritas veritati noceat*"—"Let us not fear that truth can endanger truth." If what another says is indeed true, it cannot threaten the truth that I treasure. I must open my heart and mind to the spaciousness of the divine truth. If I believe that what the other says is *not* true, I must, of course, say so, with due humility. German has the lovely word *zwischenraum*. If I understand it, it means the fullness of the space between us as we talk. It is in this empty space that the truth of God is enthroned, the space between the truths we champion. God's mystery is always revealed in empty spaces: the empty space between the wings of the cherubim on the ark of the covenant, the empty space of Mary's womb, the empty space of the cross, and the empty tomb that John tells us had angels on either side.

The clash of apparently incompatible truths can be painful and cause anger. Think of St. Paul's account of his conflict with St. Peter in Antioch as told in the letter to the Galatians: "[W]hen Cephas came to Antioch, I opposed him to his face" (2:11)! But they gave each other the right hand of fellowship, and the Holy See looks to both as founders! They were united in death as martyrs.

We must seek ways to speak the truth so that the other person can hear it without feeling demolished. Think of when Peter met Jesus on the beach, in John chapter 21. On the last evening before Jesus' death, Peter had boasted that he loved the Lord more than all the others. But shortly afterwards he denied the Lord three times, the most shameful moment in his life. On the beach, Jesus did not hammer him with his failure. He asked gently, perhaps with a smile, three times: "Do you love me more than these others?" With infinite gentleness, he helps Peter three times to undo his threefold denial. He challenges him to face the truth with all the tenderness of love. Can we challenge each other with such gentle and tender truthfulness?

The American poet Emily Dickinson gives good advice: "Tell all the truth but tell it slant— / Success in Circuit lies."[3] Forgive me for quoting poetry. It can be so hard to translate. Her point is that sometimes the truth is told most powerfully when it is done indirectly, so that the other can hear. The truth when it is shouted may be inaudible. If you tell someone that they are a patriarchal dinosaur, they probably will not be helped! Of course, it will still be painful sometimes. But Pope Francis has said, "We should not be afraid of proclaiming the truth, even if it is at times uncomfortable."[4]

This will require of us all a certain loss of control. Jesus says to Peter, "Very truly, I tell you, when you were younger, you used to fasten your own belt and to go wherever you wished. But when you grow old, you will stretch out your hands, and someone else will fasten a

3. Emily Dickinson, "Tell all the truth but tell it slant—," in *The Poems of Emily Dickinson: Reading Edition* (Cambridge, MA: The Belknap Press of Harvard University Press, 1998).

4. Pope Francis, "Message of His Holiness Pope Francis for the 57th World Day of Social Communications," January 24, 2023, https://www.vatican.va/content/francesco/en/messages/communications/documents/20230124-messaggio-comunicazioni-sociali.html.

belt around you and take you where you do not wish to go" (John 21:18).

For St. Thomas Aquinas, "Blessed are those who mourn for they shall be comforted" (Matt 5:4) is applied to those who seek the gift of knowledge. This is surely in part because if you seek to understand, you must always be letting go of old certainties as you enter into the fullness of the mystery. We let go of images of God as we draw close.

If the synod has the dynamics of prayer more than of a parliament, it will ask of us all a sort of letting go of control, even a sort of dying. Letting God be God. In *Evangelii Gaudium*, the Holy Father wrote, "[T]here is no greater freedom than that of allowing oneself to be guided by the Holy Spirit, renouncing the attempt to plan and control everything to the last detail, and instead letting him enlighten, guide and direct us, leading us wherever he wills."[5] Letting go of control is not doing nothing! Because the Church has been so much a structure of control, sometimes strong interventions are needed to let the Holy Spirit take us where we had never thought of going.

We have a profound instinct to hang on to control, which is why the synod is feared by many. At Pentecost, the Holy Spirit came powerfully upon the disciples, who were sent to the ends of the earth. But instead they

5. Pope Francis, *Evangelii Gaudium*, n. 280.

settled down in Jerusalem and did not want to leave. It took persecution to ease them out of the nest and send them away from Jerusalem! Tough love! Above my office in Santa Sabina, every year kestrels built their nest. The time came when their parents kicked the young birds out of their nest, so that they had to fly or perish. Sitting at my desk, I could see them struggling to stay in the air! The Holy Spirit sometimes kicks us out of the nest and bids us fly! We flap in panic, but fly we will! This synod is an invitation to fly!

In Gethsemane, Jesus surrenders control over his life and entrusts it to the Father. "Not as I will!" When I was a young friar, a French Dominican who had been a worker priest stayed in the community. He was going to India to serve the poorest of the poor and came to Oxford to learn Bengali. I asked him what he intended to do: "What is your plan?" He replied, "How can I know until the poor tell me?"

As a young provincial, I visited a Dominican monastery that was nearing the end. Only four ancient nuns were left. I was accompanied by the previous provincial, Peter. When we said to the nuns that future of the monastery seemed very uncertain, one of them said, "But Timothy, our dear Lord would not let our monastery die, would he?" Peter immediately replied, "Sister, he let his Son die." So we can let things die, not in despair but in hope, to give a space for the new.

So being led by the Holy Spirit means being liberated from the culture of control. In our society, leadership is all about keeping one's hands on the levers of power. Pope St. John XXIII joked that he said to God each night, "The pope must go to sleep now, and so you, God, must look after the Church for a few hours." As he understood so well, leadership is sometimes about letting go of control.

The *Instrumentum Laboris* calls us to make "the preferential option for the young" (e.g., B 2.1). Every year we remember that God came to us as a child, newborn. Confidence in the young is an intrinsic part of Christian leadership. The young are not here to take the places of us old people but to do what we cannot imagine. When St. Dominic sent his young novices out to preach, some monks warned him that he would lose them. Dominic replied, "I know for certain that my young men will go out and come back, will be sent out and will return; but your young men will be kept locked up and will still go out."[6]

Being led by the Spirit into all truth means letting go of the present, trusting that the Spirit will beget new institutions, new forms of Christian living, new ministries. Throughout the last two millennia, the Holy Spirit has been at work in creating news ways of being Church, from the desert fathers and mothers to the orders of

6. Simon Tugwell, OP, ed., *Early Dominicans: Selected Writings* (Mahwah, NJ: Paulist Press, 1982), 91.

friars in the thirteenth century, even the Jesuits during the Counter-Reformation! Hundreds of new forms of religious life sprang into being to face the challenges of the Industrial Revolution in the West. The new ecclesial movements emerged in the last century. We must let the Holy Spirit work creatively in our midst with new ways of being Church that now we cannot imagine but perhaps the young can! "Listen to him," said the voice on the mountain. That includes listening to the young in whom the Lord lives and speaks (see Matt 11:28).

Being led into the truth is not, as we have seen, *just* a matter of rational argument. We are not just brains. We open who we are, our vulnerable humanity, to each other. St. Thomas Aquinas loved a saying of Aristotle, "*Anima est quodammodo omnia*"—"The soul is, in a way, everything." We know deeply by opening our being to what is other. We let ourselves be touched and changed by encounter with each other. The fullest truth into which the Holy Spirit is leading us is not a dispassionate knowledge that inspects from a distance. It is more than propositional knowledge. It is inseparable from transformative love (see *Instrumentum Laboris* A 1.27). The Dominican way is that through knowing we come to love. The Franciscan way is that through loving, we come to know. Both are right—the Catholic *and*.

The mystery into which we are being led is of a love that is totally without rivalry. All that the Father has is given to the Son and to the Holy Spirit. Even equality. To share in the divine life is to be liberated from all rivalry and competition. It is this same divine love, freed from all rivalry, with which we should love each other during this synod. St. John wrote, "Those who say, 'I love God,' and hate their brothers or sisters, are liars; for those who do not love a brother or sister whom they have seen, cannot love God whom they have not seen" (1 John 4:20).

Profound change will come about only if the search to understand the Lord's will is entwined in the double helix of learning to love and understand those whom we find difficult. This will be hard to communicate to people who are not here. Have all these people really come all this way, at great expense, just to love each other? Practical decisions are, of course, unavoidable and necessary. But they must spring from the personal and communal transformation of who we are, otherwise they are mere administration.

What will we be given? We wait to see what the Lord in his wisdom gives, which will certainly not be what we expect. Simone Weil (1909–1943) was a French Jewish mystic who, on her journey to the truth, came to say "I believe in God, the Trinity, Redemption, the Eucharist, and the teachings of the Gospel."[7] She wrote that "we do

---

7. Simone Pétrement, *La vita di Simone Weil* (Milan: Adelphi, 2010), 646.

not obtain the most precious gifts by going in search of them but by waiting for them. . . . This way of looking is, in the first place, attentive. The soul empties itself of all its own contents in order to receive the human being it is looking at, just as he or she is, in all their truth."[8]

If we let ourselves be guided by the Spirit of truth, we shall doubtless argue. It will sometimes be painful. There will be truths we would rather not face. But we shall be led a little deeper into the mystery of divine love, and we shall know such joy that people will be envious of us for being here, and we will long to attend the next session of the synod! Even the bishop who prayed not to come this time!

8. Simone Weil, *Waiting on God*, trans. Emma Crauford (London: Routledge & Kegan Paul, 1959), 169.

Synod Meditations

The Samaritan Woman at the Well

(John 4:7-30)

October 9, 2023

A Samaritan woman came to draw water, and Jesus said to her, "Give me a drink." (His disciples had gone to the city to buy food.) The Samaritan woman said to him, "How is it that you, a Jew, ask a drink of me, a woman of Samaria?" (Jews do not share things in common with Samaritans.) Jesus answered her, "If you knew the gift of God, and who it is that is saying to you, 'Give me a drink,' you would have asked him, and he would have given you living water." The woman said to him, "Sir, you have no bucket, and the well is deep. Where do you get that living water? Are you greater than our ancestor Jacob, who gave us the well, and with his sons and his flocks drank from it?" Jesus said to her, "Everyone who drinks of this water will be thirsty again, but those who drink of the water that I will give them will never be thirsty. The water that I will give will become in them a spring of water gushing up to eternal life." The woman said to him, "Sir, give me this water, so that I may never be thirsty or have to keep coming here to draw water."

Jesus said to her, "Go, call your husband, and come back." The woman answered him, "I have no husband." Jesus said to her, "You are right in saying, 'I have no husband'; for you have had five husbands, and the one you have now is not your husband. What you have said is true!" The woman said to him, "Sir, I see that you are a prophet. Our ancestors worshiped on this mountain, but you say that the place where people must worship is in Jerusalem." Jesus said to her, "Woman, believe me, the hour is coming when you will worship the Father neither on this mountain nor in Jerusalem. You worship what you do not know; we worship what we know, for salvation is from the Jews. But the hour is coming, and is now here, when the true worshipers will worship the Father in spirit and truth, for the Father seeks such as these to worship him. God is spirit, and those who worship him must worship in spirit and truth." The woman said to him, "I know that Messiah is coming" (who is called Christ). "When he comes, he will proclaim all things to us." Jesus said to her, "I am he, the one who is speaking to you."

Just then his disciples came. They were astonished that he was speaking with a woman, but no one said, "What do you want?" or, "Why are you speaking with her?" Then the woman left her water jar and went back to the city. She said to the people, "Come and see a man who told me everything I have ever done! He cannot be the Messiah, can he?" They left the city and were on their way to him.

Meditation

Today we begin to reflect on B 1 of the *Instrumentum Laboris*, "A Communion that Radiates." The theme that emerged most frequently in our sessions last week was formation. So how can we all be formed for communion that overflows into mission?

In John chapter 4, we hear of the encounter of Jesus with the woman at the well. At the beginning of the chapter, she is alone, a solitary figure. By the end, she is transformed into the first preacher of the Gospel, just as the first preacher of the resurrection will be another woman, Mary Magdalene, the Apostle of the Apostles: two women who launch the preaching first of the good news that God has come to us and then the resurrection.

How does Jesus overcome her isolation? The encounter opens with a few short words, only three in Greek: "Give me a drink." Jesus is thirsty and for more than water. The whole of John's Gospel is structured around

Jesus' thirst. His first sign was offering wine for the thirsty guests at the wedding in Cana. Almost his last words on the cross are "I am thirsty." Then he says, "It is fulfilled" and dies.

God appears among us as one who is thirsty, above all for each of us. My student master, Geoffrey Preston, OP, wrote, "Salvation is about God longing for us and being racked with thirst for us; God wanting us so much more than we can ever want him."[1] The fourteenth-century English mystic Julian of Norwich said, "The longing and spiritual [ghostly] thirst of Christ lasts and shall last till Doomsday."[2]

God thirsted for this fallen woman so much that he became human. He shared with her what is most precious, the divine name: "I AM is the one speaking to you." It is as if the incarnation happened just for her. She learns to become thirsty, too. First of all for water, so that she need not come to the well every day. Then she discovers a deeper thirst. Until now she has gone from man to man. Now she discovers the one for whom she had always been longing without knowing it. As Romano the Melodist said, often people's erratic sex life is a fum-

1. Geoffrey Preston, OP, *Hallowing the Time: Meditations on the Cycle of the Christian Liturgy* (London: Darton, Longman and Todd, 1980), 83.

2. Julian of Norwich, *XVI Revelations of Divine Love Shewed to Mother Juliana of Norwich, 1379* (London: Kegan Paul, Trench, Trübner, 1902), 100.

bling after their deepest thirst, for God.[3] Our sins, our
failures, are usually mistaken attempts to find what we
most desire. But the Lord is waiting patiently for us by
our wells, inviting us to thirst for more.

So formation for "a communion which radiates" is
learning to thirst and hunger ever more deeply. We begin
with our ordinary desires. When I was ill with cancer in
hospital, I was not allowed to drink anything for about
three weeks. I was filled with raging thirst. Nothing ever
tasted so good as that first glass of water, even better than
a glass of whisky! But slowly I discovered that there was
a deeper thirst:

> O God, you are my God, I seek you,
>   my soul thirsts for you;
> my flesh faints for you,
> as in a dry and weary land where there is no water.
>   (Psalm 63)

What isolates us all is being trapped in small desires,
little satisfactions, such as beating our opponents or having status, wearing a special hat. According to the oral
tradition, when Thomas Aquinas was asked by his sister
Theodora how to become a saint, he replied with one

---

3. Cant. 10, quoted by Simon Tugwell, OP, *Reflections on the Beatitudes*
(London: Darton, Longman and Todd, 1980), 101.

word: *Velle*! Want it![4] Constantly Jesus asks the people who come to him, "What do you want?" "What can I do for you?" The Lord wants to give us the fullness of love. Do we want it?

So our formation for synodality means learning to become passionate people, filled with deep desire. Pedro Arrupe, the marvellous superior general of the Jesuits, wrote,

> Nothing is more practical than finding God, that is, than falling in love in a quite absolute, final way. What you are in love with, what seizes your imagination, will affect everything. It will decide what will get you out of bed in the morning, what you do with your evenings, how you spend your weekends, what you read, who you know, what breaks your heart, and what amazes you with joy and gratitude. Fall in love, stay in love, and it will decide everything.[5]

That passionate man, St. Augustine, exclaimed, "I tasted you and now hunger and thirst for you; you touched me, and I have burned for your peace."[6]

4. Placid Conway, OP, *Saint Thomas Aquinas: A Biographical Study of the Angelic Doctor* (London: Longmans, Green, 1911), 88.

5. Quoted in Virgil Elizondo, *Charity* (Maryknoll, NY: Orbis, 2008), 22.

6. *Confessions*, Bk. 10, xxvii.

But how do we become passionate people—passionate for the Gospel, filled with love for each other—without disaster? This is the fundamental question for our formation, especially for our seminarians. Jesus' love for this nameless woman sets her free. She becomes the first preacher, but we never hear of her again. A synodal Church will be one in which we are formed for unpossessive love: a love that neither flees the other person nor takes possession of them, a love that is neither abusive nor cold.

First it is an intensely personal encounter between two people. Jesus meets her as she truly is. "You are right in saying, 'I have no husband'; for you have had five husbands, and the one you have now is not your husband. What you have said is true!" She gets heated in response and replies mockingly, "Ah, so you are a prophet."

We should be formed for deeply personal encounters with each other, in which we transcend easy labels. Love is personal and hatred is abstract. I quote again from Graham Greene's novel *The Power and the Glory*: "Hate was just a failure of imagination." St. Paul's very personal disagreement with St. Peter was hard, but it was truly an encounter. The Holy See is founded on this passionate, angry, but *real* encounter. The people whom St. Paul could not abide were the underhanded spies who gossiped and worked secretly, whispering in the corridors, hiding who they were with deceitful smiles. Open disagreement was not the problem.

So many people feel excluded or marginalised in our Church because we have slapped abstract labels on them: divorced and remarried, gay people, polygamous people, refugees, Africans, Jesuits! A friend said to me the other day, "I hate labels. I hate people being put in boxes. I cannot abide these conservatives." But if you really meet someone, you may become angry, but hatred cannot be sustained in a truly personal encounter. If you glimpse their humanity, you will see the one who creates them and sustains them in being, whose name is I AM.

The foundation of our loving but unpossessive encounter with each other is surely our encounter with the Lord, each at our own well, with our failures and weaknesses and desires. He knows us as we are and sets us free to encounter each other with a love that liberates and does not control. In the silence of prayer, we are liberated.

She meets the one who knows her totally. This impels her on her mission. "Come and see the man who told me everything that I have ever done." Until now she has lived in shame and concealment, fearing the judgment of her fellow citizens. She goes to the well in the midday heat when no one else will be there. But now the Lord has shone the light on all that she is and loves her. After the Fall, Adam and Eve hide from the sight of God, ashamed. Now she steps into the light. Formation for synodality peels away our disguises and our masks, so that we step into the light. May this happen in our *circuli minori*.

Then we shall be able to mediate God's unpossessive pleasure in every one of us, in which there is no shame. I shall never forget an AIDS clinic called Mashambanzou on the edge of Harare, Zimbabwe. The word literally means "the time when elephants wash," which is the dawn. Then they go down to the river to splash around, squirt water over themselves and each other. It is a time of joy and play. Most of the patients were teenagers who did not have long to live, but it is a place of joy. I especially remember one young lad called Courage, who filled the place with laughter.

In Phnom Penh, Cambodia, I visited another AIDS hospice run by a priest called Jim. He and his helpers collect people who are dying of AIDS in the streets and bring them back to this simple wooden hut. One young man had just been brought in. He was emaciated and did not look as if he had long to live. They were washing and cutting his hair. His face was blissful. This was God's child in whom the Father delights.

The disciples returned with food. They were shocked to see Jesus talking to this fallen woman. Wells are places of romantic encounter in the Bible! As with her, their conversation with him had a slow beginning—two words only: "Rabbi, eat" (John 4:31). But she became a preacher even before them. Our role as priests is often to support those who have already begun to reap the harvest before we even wake up.

The Council of Jerusalem
(Acts 15:1-29)

October 18, 2023

Then certain individuals came down from Judea and were teaching the brothers, "Unless you are circumcised according to the custom of Moses, you cannot be saved." And after Paul and Barnabas had no small dissension and debate with them, Paul and Barnabas and some of the others were appointed to go up to Jerusalem to discuss this question with the apostles and the elders. So they were sent on their way by the church, and as they passed through both Phoenicia and Samaria, they reported the conversion of the Gentiles, and brought great joy to all the believers. When they came to Jerusalem, they were welcomed by the church and the apostles and the elders, and they reported all that God had done with them. But some believers who belonged to the sect of the Pharisees stood up and said, "It is necessary for them to be circumcised and ordered to keep the law of Moses."

The apostles and the elders met together to consider this matter. After there had been much debate, Peter stood up and said to them, "My brothers, you know that in the early days God made a choice among you, that I should be the one through whom the Gentiles would hear the message of the good news and become believers. And God, who knows the human heart, testified to them by giving them the Holy Spirit, just as he did to us; and in cleansing their hearts by faith he has made no distinction between them and us. Now therefore why are you putting God to the test by placing on the neck of the disciples a yoke that neither our ancestors nor we have been able to bear? On the contrary, we believe that we will be saved through the grace of the Lord Jesus, just as they will."

The whole assembly kept silence, and listened to Barnabas and Paul as they told of all the signs and wonders that God had done through them among the Gentiles. After they finished speaking, James replied, "My brothers, listen to me. Simeon has related how God first looked favorably on the Gentiles, to take from among them a people for his name. This agrees with the words of the prophets, as it is written,

'After this I will return,
and I will rebuild the dwelling of David, which
   has fallen;
   from its ruins I will rebuild it,
      and I will set it up,
so that all other peoples may seek the Lord—
   even all the Gentiles over whom my name has
      been called.
      Thus says the Lord, who has been making
         these things
   known from long ago.'

Therefore I have reached the decision that we should not trouble those Gentiles who are turning to God, but we should write to them to abstain only from things polluted by idols and from fornication and from whatever has been strangled and from blood. For in every city, for generations past, Moses has had those who proclaim him, for he has been read aloud every sabbath in the synagogues."

Then the apostles and the elders, with the consent of the whole church, decided to choose men from among their members and to send them to Antioch with Paul and Barnabas. They sent Judas called Barsabbas, and Silas, leaders among the brothers, with the following letter: "The brothers, both the apostles and the elders, to the believers of Gentile origin in Antioch and Syria and Cilicia, greetings. Since we have heard that certain persons

who have gone out from us, though with no instruc-
tions from us, have said things to disturb you and have
unsettled your minds, we have decided unanimously
to choose representatives and send them to you, along
with our beloved Barnabas and Paul, who have risked
their lives for the sake of our Lord Jesus Christ. We have
therefore sent Judas and Silas, who themselves will tell
you the same things by word of mouth. For it has seemed
good to the Holy Spirit and to us to impose on you no
further burden than these essentials: that you abstain
from what has been sacrificed to idols and from blood
and from what is strangled and from fornication. If you
keep yourselves from these, you will do well. Farewell."

Meditation

So: "Participation, government and authority: What processes, structures and institutions are needed in a missionary synodal Church?" (*Instrumentum Laboris* B 3).

Luke, whose feast we celebrate today, tells us in Acts
15 about the so-called Council of Jerusalem, called to
face the first great crisis of the Church after Pentecost.
The Church was profoundly fractured. First, there was
the fracture between the Jerusalem Church and Paul,
with his Gospel of freedom from the law. But also within
the Jerusalem Church, the convert Pharisees were divided from the rest, and the apostles led by Peter were

probably divided from the "elders" who looked to James, the brother of the Lord. So the Church faced a crisis of identity that exceeded anything we can imagine today.

Pope Francis said at Lisbon this summer, "A life without crises is a sterilized life. . . . A life without crisis is like distilled water. It has no flavour. It has no purpose."[1] We mature through crises, from the crisis of our birth to the crisis of death. If we embrace crises in hope, we shall flourish. If we try to avoid them, we shall never grow up. My American brethren gave me a T-shirt that said, "Have a good crisis!"

We read that "the apostles and the elders gathered together to consider this matter" (Acts 15:6). The Church is always being gathered, as we are today in the synod. In Eucharistic Prayer III, we say, "[Y]ou never cease to gather a people to yourself, so that from the rising of the sun to its setting a pure sacrifice may be offered to your name." The Greek word for the Church, *ekklesia*, means "gathering," across space and time. Are we willing to be gathered together, not just physically, but with our hearts and minds, too? Gazing at Jerusalem before his death,

1. Pope Francis, "Meeting with Young People of Scholas Occurrentes, Greeting of His Holiness," Apostolic Journey of His Holiness Pope Francis to Portugal on the Occasion of the XXXVII World Youth Day, August 3, 2023, https://www.vatican.va/content/francesco/en/speeches/2023/august/documents/20230803-portogallo-scholas-occurrentes.html.

Jesus said, "How often have I desired to gather your children together as a hen gathers her brood under her wing, but you were not willing!" (Matt 23:37). Are we willing to be drawn beyond mutual incomprehension and suspicion? Or shall we be like the elder brother in the parable of the Prodigal Son who stands on the edge, refusing to be gathered into the joy of his brother's return?

The disciples gathered in Jerusalem so as to be sent out to Antioch and the whole world. We are gathered in the Eucharist so as to be sent out. This is the breathing of the Holy Spirit in our lungs, gathering us in and sending us out, oxygenating the lifeblood of the Church. Our peace should be a witness to our poor world, crucified by ever more violence, in Ukraine, the Holy Land, Myanmar, Sudan, and so many other places. How can we be a sign of peace if we are angrily divided among ourselves?

The Council of Jerusalem gathered "in the name of Jesus," as we are, too. In the synod we pray every day, "We stand before you, Holy Spirit, as we gather *in your name*." To be gathered in the name of the Lord means in the sure confidence that God's grace is powerfully at work within us. Peter said to the lame man by the temple gate: "I have neither silver or gold, but what I have I give you; in the name of Jesus Christ of Nazareth, stand up and walk" (Acts 3:6). Often people have told me, "This synod will not change anything." Some say it with hope and some with fear. That is a lack of faith in the name of the Lord, "the name / that is above every name" (Phil 2:9). An ancient hymn begins, "I bind unto myself today, the strong name of the Trinity." If we are gathered in the strong name of the Trinity, the Church *will* be renewed, though maybe not in ways that are immediately obvious or in ways that we want. This is not optimism but our apostolic faith.

My first great teacher was a Sri Lankan Dominican, Cornelius Ernst. He wrote of the power of God's grace to make new: "It is dawn, discovery, spring, new birth, coming to the light, awakening, transcendence, liberation, ecstasy, bridal consent, gift, forgiveness, reconciliation, revolution, faith, hope, love. . . . It is the power to transform and renew all things: 'Behold I make all things new' (Apoc. 21.5)."[2] The Church is always old and new, like God, the Ancient of Days and the newborn child.

The disciples gathered because they recognised that God was *already* doing something new. God had gone before them. They had to catch up with the Holy Spirit. Peter proclaimed that "God, who knows the human heart, testified to them by giving them the Holy Spirit, just as he did to us; and in cleansing their hearts by faith he has made no distinction between them and us" (Acts 15:8-9).

2. Cornelius Ernst, OP, *The Theology of Grace*, Theology Today Series, vol. 17 (Dublin: Fides, 1974), 74–75.

This was surely hardest for St. James, the brother of the Lord, to accept. His identity was founded on a blood relationship with the Lord. It is marvellous that *he* is the one who proclaims this new identity. "It has seemed good to the Holy Spirit and to *us*." What courage and faith it must have taken to say "us," an identity that gathers in all of the divided Church. He still called Peter by his old family name, Simeon. He was awakening only slowly to this new identity, a Church of Jews and Gentiles. It took time, as it does for us.

During the civil war in Burundi, I toured the country with two of my brothers, a Hutu and a Tutsi. At night the three of us celebrated the Eucharist together. One Englishman and two Africans, a Hutu and a Tutsi: a new sense of *we*. We received it in the Eucharist before we grasped it in our minds and hearts.

Today our God is already bringing into existence a Church that is no longer primarily Western: a Church that is Eastern Catholic and Asian and African and Latin American. It is a Church in which already women are assuming responsibility and are renewing our theology and spirituality. Already young people all over the world, as we saw at Lisbon, are taking us in new directions, into the digital continent. In the Sacramentary, in the Preface for Holy Men and Women, we thank God because "[y]ou renew the Church in every age by raising up men and women outstanding in holiness." They are already among us. We rightly ask: What shall we do? An even more fundamental question is: What is *God* doing? Do we rightly discern what God is doing and what is not of God? Can you believe, some Dominicans even opposed St. Ignatius of Loyola and the foundation of the Society! *Nostra culpa.*

Fascinatingly, James can only understand the new as a rebuilding of the old. He cites Amos:

> "After this I will return,
> and I will rebuild the dwelling of David, which
>   has fallen;
>   from its ruins I will rebuild it,
>   and I will set it up,
> so that all other peoples may seek the Lord—
>   even all the Gentiles over whom my name has
> been called." (Acts 15:16-17)

The new is always an unexpected renewal of the old. This is why any opposition between tradition and progress is utterly alien to Catholicism.

Now we shall consider what new processes, institutions, and structures are needed. These will not be solutions to management problems but fuller expressions of who we are. The history of the Church is of endless institutional creativity. After Christianity became a recognised religion of the Roman Empire, new forms of Christian life emerged in the desert fathers and mothers, to counterbalance the new dangers of wealth. In the thirteenth century, new universities emerged to explore a new vision of what it is to be human. During the Industrial Revolution, hundreds of new forms of religious life sprang into being, to express who we are as brothers and sisters of the new urban poor.

What institutions do we need to express who we are as men and women of peace in an age of violence, inhabitants of the digital continent? Every baptised person is a prophet. How do we recognise and embrace the role of prophecy in the Church today?[3] What about the prophetic voice of women, still often seen as "guests in their own house"[4]?

Finally, the Council of Jerusalem lifted unnecessary burdens from the Gentiles. "For it has seemed good to the Holy Spirit and to us to impose on you no further burden than these essentials" (Acts 15:28). They are freed from an identity given by the old Law.

How shall we lift burdens from the weary shoulders of our brothers and sisters today? It will not be through anything as dramatic as abolishing the Law. Nor will it

3. Massimo Faggioli, "Notes on Prophecy and the Ecclesiology of Synodality from the Second Vatican Council to Today," *Irish Theological Quarterly* 88, no. 4 (November 2023): 308–22.

4. Carmel McEnroy, *Guests in Their Own House: The Women of Vatican II* (New York: Crossroad, 2011).

be through such a fundamental shift in our identity as the admission of the Gentiles.

But we are called to embrace a deeper sense of who we are as the improbable friends of the Lord, whose scandalous friendship reaches across every boundary. Many of us wept when we heard of that young woman who committed suicide because she was bisexual and did not feel welcomed. I did. I hope it changed us. The Holy Father reminded us that all are welcomed: *todos, todos, todos.*

A man was lost in Ireland. He asked a farmer, "How do I get to Dublin?" The farmer replied, "If I wanted to go to Dublin, I would not start here." But wherever people are, that is where the journey home starts, the home of the Church and the home of the kingdom.

The Seed Germinates
(Mark 4:27-29)

October 23, 2023

[J esus] also said, "The kingdom of God is as if someone would scatter seed on the ground, and would sleep and rise night and day, and the seed would sprout and grow, he does not know how. The earth produces of itself, first the stalk, then the head, then the full grain in the head. But when the grain is ripe, at once he goes in with his sickle, because the harvest has come."

Meditation

In a few days' time, we shall go home for eleven months. This will be apparently a time of empty waiting. But it

113

will probably be the most fertile time of the synod, the time of germination. Jesus tells us, "The kingdom of God is as if someone would scatter seed on the ground, and would sleep and rise night and day, and the seed would sprout and grow, he does not know how."

We have listened to hundreds of thousands of words during the last three weeks. Sometimes we may have thought, "Too many!" Most of these have been positive words, words of hope and aspiration. These are the seeds that are sown in the soil of the Church. They will be at work in our lives, in our imagination and our subconscious, during these months. When the moment is right, they will bear fruit.

The Austrian poet Rainer Maria Rilke wrote:

> In spite of all the farmer's work and worry,
> He can't reach down to where the seed is slowly
> 'Transmuted into summer'. The earth bestows.[1]

Although nothing may appear to be happening, we can be confident that if our words are loving, they will bud in the lives of people whom we do not know. As St. Thérèse of Lisieux said, as quoted by the Holy Father recently:

1. Rainer Maria Rilke, "The Sonnets to Orpheus XII," in *Selected Poems: With Parallel German Text*, trans. Susan Ranson and Marielle Sutherland (Oxford: Oxford University Press, 2011), 195.

"C'est la confiance et rien que la confiance qui doit nous conduire à l'Amour"—"It is confidence and nothing but confidence that must lead us to Love."[2]

These eleven months will be like a pregnancy. Abraham and Sarah were promised that they would have descendants more numerous than the sand on the seashore. But nothing seemed to happen. Sarah laughed when she heard this promise the third or fourth time, as she listened, hidden in the tent, to the strangers in Genesis 18. Probably a bittersweet laugh. She had heard all this before, but she had remained barren. But in a year's time, she would bear Isaac, the child of laughter.

So these eleven months will be a time of quiet pregnancy, of a new way of being Church, a deeper communion. If you will forgive me, this reminds me of the first time I tried to make a speech in Spanish, in Latin America. A bishop got confused—which is very rare. He thought that I was an Irish Franciscan. I explained that I was an English Dominican. I said, *"El obispo esta embarazado."* I meant to say, "The bishop was embarrassed."

2. St. Thérèse of the Child Jesus and the Holy Face, Letter 197 to Sister Marie of the Sacred Heart (September 17, 1896), *Letters II: 1890–1897* (Washington, DC: ICS Publications, 1988), 1000; see Pope Francis, Apostolic Exhortation *C'est La Confiance*, October 15, 2023, https://www.vatican.va/content/francesco/en/apost_exhortations/documents/20231015-santateresa-delbambinogesu.html.

Alas, what I actually said was, "The bishop is pregnant." Even more rare!

This is a time of active waiting. Let me repeat the words of Simone Weil that I quoted during the retreat. "We do not obtain the most precious gifts by going in search of them but by waiting for them. . . . This way of looking is, in the first place, attentive. The soul empties itself of all its own contents in order to receive the human being it is looking at, just as he or she is, in all their truth."[3]

This is profoundly countercultural. The global culture of our time is often polarised, aggressive, and dismissive of other people's views. The cry is: Whose side are you on? When we go home, people will ask, "Did you fight for our side? Did you oppose those unenlightened other people?" We shall need be profoundly prayerful to resist the temptation to succumb to this party-political way of thinking. That would be to fall back into the sterile, barren language of much of our society. It is not the synodal way.

The synodal process is organic and ecological rather than competitive. It is more like planting a tree than winning a battle (though battles are sometimes unavoidable, as St. Athanasius knew so well!), and as such will be hard for many to understand, sometimes including ourselves (see Mark 8:33)!

3. Weil, *Waiting on God*, 169.

But if we keep our minds and hearts open to the people whom we have met here, vulnerable to their hopes and fears, their words will germinate in our lives, and ours in theirs. There will an abundant harvest, a fuller truth. Then the Church will be renewed.

Humanity's first vocation in Paradise was to be gardeners. Adam tended creation, given a share in speaking God's creative words, naming the animals. In these eleven months, will we speak fertile, hope-filled words, or words that are destructive and cynical? Will our words nurture the crop or be poisonous? Shall we be gardeners of the future or trapped in old, sterile conflicts? We each choose.

St. Paul said to the Ephesians: "Let no evil talk come out of your mouths, but only what is useful for building up, as there is need, so that your words may give grace to those who hear" (4:29).

Go!

"Now the LORD said to Abram, 'Go from your country and your kindred and your father's house to the land that I will show you'" (Gen 12:1). Summoned out of Egypt into the wilderness on the way to the Promised Land; called back home from Babylonian exile; journeying with Jesus to Jerusalem, the first synod—the risen Lord sends us with another "Go": "Go therefore and make disciples of all nations" (Matt 28:19). At the end of every Eucharist, we are told to "go in peace." We hope to hear that final summons: "Come, you that are blessed by my Father, inherit the kingdom prepared for you from the foundation of the world" (Matt 25:34). Discipleship is a journey into the mystery of God. The only question is whether we accept to travel together (*syn-hodos*).

"It is the LORD who goes before you. He will be with you; he will not fail you or forsake you. Do not fear or be dismayed" (Deut 31:8).

The media, both mainstream and "independent" Catholic media, mostly concluded that during this first session of the Synod on Synodality, the Church did not make any significant progress. The Synthesis Report was greeted with disappointment. The Church was asked for the third time to study the issue of ordaining women to the diaconate. Pope Francis has constantly urged the Church to welcome everyone—"*todos, todos, todos*"—but the Synthesis Report retreated from explicitly naming the LGBT community, which both Pope Francis and the preparatory document had done previously. Rather than going anywhere, it seemed that the Church is aimlessly wandering around in the wilderness, like the people of God after the exodus.

The downbeat reaction of the media initially irritated me. It had been made clear from the beginning that the purpose of this session of the synod was not to make audacious decisions. In my first retreat talk, I had said that "the media will probably decide that it was all a waste of time, just words. They will look for whether bold decisions are made on about four or five hot-button topics." Hadn't they listened? But I had to admit that I, too, was a little disappointed! So many people would feel discouraged, especially women who were waiting to see whether we had responded to their desire to have a strong voice

in the Church. Some of them have been hanging on by
their fingernails. How would they bear the news?

The hope for tangible, structural changes in the life
of our Church is valid. I share it and pray for it. But
even after a month in synod, it was easy to forget that
the transformation that it *is* bringing about is far more
radical than we can easily grasp. It is a new way of being
Church, a deeper sharing in the life of Christ and in the
communion of the Trinity. It is from that communion
that structural changes will come when the time is ripe.
Doing springs from being, from our encounter with the
one whose name is I AM. If that is not the foundation,
we shall just be shifting the deck chairs on the ecclesiastical *Titanic*.

The Church is the community born of the living encounter with the Lord.

> The way in which Jesus formed the disciples con-
> stitutes the model we need to follow. He did not
> merely impart teaching but he shared his life with
> them. . . . He makes new life possible with his
> presence: those who meet him come away trans-
> formed. This happens because the truth of which
> Jesus is the bearer is not an idea, but the very pres-
> ence of God in our midst; and the love with which
> he acts is not just a feeling, but the justice of the
> Kingdom that changes history. (Synthesis Report
> 14 b, 15 f)

The foundation of everything that happened in those four weeks was prayer: the Eucharist and shared silence in which we listened to the Lord and to each other. We were invited to see each other not as rivals with competing visions of the Church but as fellow disciples walking with the Lord. In his opening address, Cardinal Jean-Claude Hollerich, the general relator of the synod, offered us this image:

> It is only normal that there is a group walking at His right, another at His left, while some run ahead and others lag behind. When each of these groups looks at Christ our Lord, together with Him they cannot help but see the group that is doing the opposite: those walking on the right will see those walking on the left, those running ahead will see those lagging behind. In other words, the so-called progressive cannot look at Christ without seeing the so-called conservatives with Him and vice-versa. Nevertheless, the important thing is not the group to which we seem to belong, but walking with Christ within His Church.[1]

1. Cardinal Jean-Claude Hollerich, SJ, "Speech by His Eminence Cardinal Jean-Claude Hollerich, SJ," October 4, 2023, Holy See Press Office, https://press.vatican.va/content/salastampa/en/bollettino /pubblico/2023/10/04/231004e.html.

Conversations Leading to Conversion

These encounters with each other principally took place in the "conversations in the Spirit" at the round tables at which all the members of the synod were seated. As an assistant to the synod, I did not take part in these conversations, and so let me quote someone who did, Father James Martin, SJ:

> Everyone went around the table and for three minutes (strictly timed) shared their response to the question at hand. Our questions came from the working document, or *Instrumentum Laboris*—for example, "How can a synodal church make credible the promise that 'love and truth will meet'?" No one could interrupt and everyone had to listen. That meant that the cardinal-archbishop of an ancient archdiocese listened to a 19-year-old college student from Wyoming. Or the patriarch or primate of a country listened to a woman theology professor. No interruptions, responses or talkbacks at this stage.
>
> In the second round, after more prayer, we shared what we had heard, what moved us and what resonances we felt in the discussion. Where was the Spirit moving? Again, no interruptions. I was at tables where the facilitator (it helps to have them) would say, "Cardinal, she hasn't finished yet." Finally, the third session was a freer discussion,

> where we could answer questions, share experiences and challenge one another.[2]

Even sitting on the edge, I saw the smiles and the laughter, barriers falling. Does it sound crazy to assert that one of the fruits of this first part of the synod was that people who had regarded each other with mutual incomprehension were learning to smile at each other? This is the beginning of all Christian ministry. I am writing this on the feast of St. Martin de Porres, OP, whose smile was at the heart of his sanctity: "His smile gave courage to the timid, comfort to sufferers, confidence to those who faltered, hope to the oppressed. Most important of all, it always aroused distaste for evil and love of good."[3] Smiles begot smiles. Kind deeds beget others. During the synod, Luca Casarini told us of how a young refugee, whom he saved by pulling him from the Mediterranean, went on to save someone who was drowning in a canal in Venice.

The war was raging in Ukraine when the synod began, and on the fourth day of our meeting, Hamas launched its horrifying attack on Israel. We saw haunting images of young people whose lives were snuffed out by

2. James Martin, SJ, "What Happened at the Synod on Synodality," *America*, October 30, 2023, https://www.americamagazine.org/faith/2023/10/30/synod-synodality-james-martin-246399.

3. Giuliana Cavallini, *St. Martin De Porres: Apostle of Charity* (St. Louis, MO: B. Herder, 1963), 44.

violence. When the future of so many young people was in jeopardy, the synod was asked to make a preferential option for the young. The youngest participant was a nineteen-year-old American. These will be the bearers of hope for the future and our missionaries in the digital continent. Austin Ivereigh puts it well: "Here is the new Galilee, where people seek God in the liquid, plural, parallel world where we now spend so much of our time."[4]

So this month of prayer and conversation deeply touched and changed most of those present. I had been a member of three previous synods and was often treated with suspicion and even hostility by members of the Roman Curia, with the exception of Cardinal Ratzinger, who was unfailingly friendly. What a change now! With the exception of a very small number of people who kept their distance, I was caught up in the joy and warmth of a community that was open to the fresh breathing of the Spirit. This was difficult to convey to the media.

The Vocation of the Catholic Media

Pope Benedict once said of the Second Vatican Council:

> There was the Council of the Fathers—the real Council—but there was also the Council of the

4. Austin Ivereigh, "How the Synod Will Change the Church," *The Tablet*, November 11, 2023, 6.

media. It was almost a Council apart, and the world perceived the Council through the latter, through the media. Thus, the Council that reached the people with immediate effect was that of the media, not that of the Fathers. And while the Council of the Fathers was conducted within the faith—it was a Council of faith seeking *intellectus*, seeking to understand itself and seeking to understand the signs of God at that time, seeking to respond to the challenge of God at that time and to find in the word of God a word for today and tomorrow— while all the Council, as I said, moved within the faith, as *fides quaerens intellectum*, the Council of the journalists, naturally, was not conducted within the faith, but within the categories of today's media, namely apart from faith, with a different hermeneutic. It was a political hermeneutic: for the media, the Council was a political struggle, a power struggle between different trends in the Church. It was obvious that the media would take the side of those who seemed to them more closely allied with their world.[5]

In a similar way, the media mostly misunderstood the synod, seeing it through the lens of a struggle for power.

5. Pope Benedict XVI, "Meeting with the Parish Priests and the Clergy of Rome: Address of Pope Benedict XVI," February 14, 2013, https://www.vatican.va/content/benedict-xvi/en/speeches/2013/february/documents/hf_ben-xvi_spe_20130214_clero-roma.html.

My meditation on the Council of Jerusalem was reported by one journalist as championing gay rights, which must have demanded a remarkable determination to get me wrong. I was consoled by the American singer Taylor Swift, who experienced relentless attacks in the media ("haters gonna hate") and responded with plucky courage: "Shake it off! Shake it off!" Even the final Synthesis Report was seen by some in competitive terms. Someone remarked that "the progressives got the process and the conservatives got the content." But, as Marshall McLuhan liked to repeat, "The medium is the message." Of course, there was conflict and tension in the synod hall. If there had not been, the synod would not have been necessary. But the process of mutual, prayerful listening summoned us beyond rival camps to walk together, which indeed we began to do. A new sense of *we* is beginning to emerge.

To protect our freedom to move beyond entrenched positions, the Holy Father asked us to observe "a diet of silence." This was not a total ban on communication. Meditations and documents were shared, interviews were recorded, and there were press briefings every day. But the conversations in which members of the synod tentatively opened themselves to each other needed shelter from the "culture wars," which reduce every exchange to a political clash. Even the members of synod, myself included, are so penetrated by the aggressive culture of our time that it was hard to hang onto what was happening most profoundly in our midst, the working of the Holy Spirit's grace at the core of our being. So it is unsurprising that the media often concluded that nothing of interest was happening.

In the end, we *have* to relate to the media. Thomas Reese, SJ, reminded us that we must "feed the beast or the beast eats you."[6] If we regard the media as "the enemy," we shall remain locked in a small ecclesiastical bubble. This is why the Catholic media has a religious (one might even say "priestly") vocation of fundamental importance, mediating to the Church and the world a glimpse of this meeting as an event of faith. Many journalists did so admirably and for them we should be grateful.[7]

"[He] emptied himself, / taking the form of a slave" (Phil 2:7).

From the beginning of his pontificate, Pope Francis has denounced clericalism as the curse that poisons our encounter with each other in the Lord, the utter negation of synodality. At the end of the synod, he repeated: "Cleri-

6. Thomas J. Reese, "What Pope Francis Forgot about the Media: You Either Feed the Beast or the Beast Eats You," *America*, October 20, 2023, https://www.americamagazine.org/faith/2023/10/20/synod-synodality -media-246340.

7. Christopher Lamb deserves an honourable mention, for example, for his excellent article, "The Church Begins to Dream," *The Tablet*, November 4, 2023.

calism is a thorn, it is a scourge, it is a form of worldliness that defiles and damages the face of the Lord's bride [the Church]; it enslaves the holy, faithful people of God."[8] The Synthesis Report defined clericalism as "a misunderstanding of the divine call, conceiving this more as a privilege than a service, and which is manifested as a refusal to be held accountable" (11 c). Such a poisonous culture must surely have been a factor in the scandal of sexual abuse, a betrayal of Jesus' call to equal friendship.

I share unreservedly Pope Francis's distaste for clericalism. I joined the Dominicans because I felt called to be one of the brethren. I nervously accepted ordination to the priesthood because my brethren wished it. I discovered the beauty of priesthood in the sacrament of reconciliation, in which I had the joy of receiving the liberation of mercy side by side with fellow sinners.

It was hard to imagine escape from clericalism in the shadow of St. Peter's Basilica, a triumphalist assertion of priestly and papal power. Every new moment in the synod was initiated with a Mass at the altar of the Chair of St. Peter, victorious over the enemies of the Church. I was reassured by the sight of St. Dominic to

8. Pope Francis, "Intervention of the Holy Father at the 18th General Congregation of the 16th Ordinary General Assembly of the Synod of Bishops," October 25, 2023, Holy See Press Office, https://press.vatican .va/content/salastampa/en/bollettino/pubblico/2023/10/25/231025f.html.

the right of the altar with his very unclerical dog peering inquisitively at us all. We entered the Paul VI Hall passing between the gorgeously dressed Swiss Guards. When cardinals and bishops were called on to speak, extravagant ecclesiastical titles rang out—Most Reverend Eminences, Excellencies, and Monsignors. We were delighted when the next speaker was announced as "Sua Eccellenza, Monsignore Robert Barron," but the puzzled face of Sister Mary Barron popped up on the screen. Of course, the Church is a hierarchical institution. No community can exist without hierarchy, not even a football team, but signs and symbols of clerical status saturated the atmosphere. How in this context could we imagine a Church that is cleansed of clericalist elitism and in which is the equal dignity of all of the baptised shines forth?

We need a shared vision of the true beauty of the ministerial priesthood, a vocation that a priest may cherish and, yes, of which he should be proud. Clericalism is a perversion of what is good, an indispensable dimension of the life of the people of God. Without the skeleton of the hierarchy, the people of God would collapse into an amorphous jellyfish and disappear. The Synthesis Report affirmed that "there is a need to find ways to involve the clergy (deacons, priests, bishops) more actively in the synodal process during the course of the next year. A synodal Church cannot do without their voices, experiences or contributions. We need to understanding belter the reasons why some have felt resistant to the synodal process" (1 n). Many bishops and priests feel lonely, isolated, unappreciated. For some the synod seems like a threat. Unless we can find cherishing their vocation (mine too!), we shall not progress along the synodal path.

This is not the moment to offer a renewed theology of the priesthood, and I am not the person to do so, but surely we need to imagine how being *in persona Christi*—acting in the person of Christ—does not so much set priests and bishops apart as root them in the midst of the flock, immersing them in the joys and sorrows of their people. The "ontological change" of ordination, to use the technical language, means that in the depths of their being, they become profoundly related to others. Their being is for others. To preside at the Eucharist—"This is my body, given for you"—is to give away your life. The Synthesis Report called for the formation of seminarians so that they "remain connected to the daily life of the community" (11 e).

Once when visiting a gathering of tribal people in the north of Pakistan, I suddenly spotted their priest, an American Dominican, sitting on the ground in the midst of his people, wearing their clothes and doubtless "smelling of his sheep," as Pope Francis likes to say. Yes, I thought, that is what priesthood looks like.

This is a synod of bishops. These 169 bishops were gathered in collegiality *cum Petro et sub Petro*. Being

seated at round tables with lay people and religious, immersed in the conversation of the people of God, did
not diminish the episcopal nature of the gathering but
made it more manifest than at any previous synod I have
attended, where the massed ranks of purple skullcaps
were set apart.

"O brave new world that has such people in it"[9]

On October 27, at the end of a Day of Fasting for Peace,
during the recitation of the rosary, Pope Francis said,
"This is a dark hour." The synod gathered people from
Russia and Ukraine, delegates of Arab and Jewish de-
scent. Our brothers and sisters also came from places of
war such as Myanmar, South Sudan, and the Democratic
Republic of the Congo. We Westerners often understood
the synod in terms of our agenda. Would the Church in
Europe or America be reformed as we wished? I expect
most of us came to the synod with our own list of hot-
button topics that we wanted addressed. But, without
in any way downplaying the importance of these issues,
isn't there a danger of a sort of "autoreferentiality," to
use Pope Francis's word, a self-centredness? Synodality
is about holy conversations that lead to conversion. As
we listened to our brothers and sisters from Africa, Latin

9. William Shakespeare, *The Tempest*, Act 5, Scene 1.

America, and Asia during those four weeks, many of us awoke to more radical questions. What does it mean to be one in the Body of Christ with those whose lands and people are consumed by war? How far are our own countries complicit in the corruption that subverts their peace and prosperity?

After the fall of the Berlin Wall in 1989, the world seemed to have left behind the bitter polarization of the Cold War. In 1992, Francis Fukuyama published *The End of History and the Last Man*,[10] arguing that we had entered a new era, the triumph of Western liberal democracy. Other prominent thinkers, included anthropologist Claude Lévi-Strauss, had a similar view. Every nation seemed destined to "evolve" into our way of life. Some countries, especially in the global South, just had to catch up, it was assumed. We had gone ahead. If they did not agree with us on, for example, the welcome of LGBT people, they would surely do so eventually.

Thirty years after the publication of Fukuyama's book, it is evident that this was an illusion. We are entering a new multipolar world. China's Belt and Road Initiative of 2013 is a global infrastructure development that involves one hundred fifty countries and three quarters of the world's population. This is to be the new Silk Road.

10. Francis Fukuyama, *The End of History and the Last Man* (London: Penguin, 1992).

The West can no longer assume that we are the point of reference for most of the world's population. Our world is seen as in decline, with fading influence. Many nations in the developing world did not react with horror to Russia's invasion of Ukraine as the West had expected and rush to support Western resistance. Reactions to the conflict in the Middle East questioned our assumptions as to how the world is seen.

The synod gathered people who see the future of humanity very differently. Westerners might see themselves as standard-bearers of the future, but for many others, the West is still a colonial power. Racism persists. Who are we in the West to assume that we are the only ones to show the way forward? Our churches are emptying, vocations to the priesthood and religious life are diminishing, and so others ask who are we to tell those whose churches are flourishing how to behave? Our hot-button topics are not those of Christians whose nations are being consumed by poverty and violence. LGBT rights are seen by some parts of the world as symptomatic of a failing Western ideology that we have no right to impose on the rest of the world.

So in this synod we were faced with a question, the answer to which is not yet clear. In this emerging multipolar world, what does it mean for the Church to be one and Catholic? During the first Iraqi War (1990–1991), the Dominican family organised a monthlong fast for peace in Union Square, New York. We gave out bumper stickers: "We have family in Iraq," and not just Dominican brothers and sisters. What might be the cost be of really seeing our brothers and sisters in Syria or the Congo as flesh of our flesh? Isaiah asks what fast the Lord wants: "When you see the naked, to cover them and not to hide yourself from your own kin?" (Isa 58:7). What might be the wonderful blessings of opening our eyes to see brothers and sisters who will bless us in ways we could never have anticipated?

With the United Nations largely, alas, seen as ineffectual, what other institution could possibly represent the call to universal fraternity? *Fratelli Tutti*! In a world drifting towards disintegration, the rise of dictatorships and the crumbling of democracies, in the Paul VI Hall we glimpsed a small and fragile sign of hope for humanity, called to be one in Christ and to share in the unity of our triune God. We have barely begun to grasp what this might mean and what a beacon of light it might be.

Was there any evidence of this in the Synthesis Report that was approved at the end of this first stage of the synod? Yes, I believe so. A young Italian Dominican, Giovanni Castellano, wrote that "the purpose of this assembly was not to say 'yes' or 'no' to the female diaconate or to abolish priestly celibacy, but to help build a Church where these questions that touch the hearts of many believers *can and must* be asked."[11] Despite the vast differences between our cultures, the assembly agreed

11. Giovanni Castellano, OP, "Was This Synod a Waste of Time?," Dominican Dispatches substack, November 5, 2023.

overwhelmingly that these questions must indeed be asked and some of them answered before we meet again.

Let me repeat C. S. Lewis's claim that while lovers look at each other, friends look in the same direction, sharing the same questions: "'Do you *care about* the same truth?' The [one] who agrees with us that some question, little regarded by others, is of great importance, can be our Friend. He need not agree with us about the answer."[12] The synod may not have arrived as of yet at shared conclusions, but we have begun to share the same questions. This is the basis for a Gospel friendship that is unparalleled anywhere else today.

The question of ordination of women to the diaconate raises complex questions of gender identity, understood very differently in our different cultures. Have we the courage and intelligence to listen profoundly to each other, seeking the truth that may lie beyond all of our perceptions? When one prominent critic, not in the synod, dismissed Pope Francis's views on the Church and gender as "misogynistic drivel," my heart sank with immense sadness. What a stark refusal to take the synodal path and listen to each other with respect even when one disagrees.

Most Catholics in the West differ from our brothers and sisters elsewhere in how we view the place of LGBT

12. Lewis, *The Four Loves*, 66.

people in the Church. The topic has become emblematic of the Church's response to Pope Francis's call that *all* should be welcome. All! Despite our difference, the assembly voted almost without dissent on this proposition:

> In different ways, people who feel marginalized or excluded from the Church because of their marriage status, identity or sexuality also ask to be heard and accompanied. There was a deep sense of love, mercy and compassion felt in the Assembly for those who are or feel hurt or neglected by the Church, who want a place to call "home" where they can feel safe, be heard and respected, without fear of feeling judged. Listening is a prerequisite for walking together in search of God's will. The Assembly reiterates that Christians must always show respect for the dignity of every person. (Synthesis Report 16 h)

In many countries from which the members of the synod came, homosexuality remains a crime punished with death. That such a statement was accepted almost with unanimity is a marvellous sign of convergence. James Martin, SJ, again: "The real message of the synod is the synod itself: how we came together to discuss difficult topics. And I was amazed that the topic was discussed so openly and so extensively in the synod, surely a major step forward in the Church, along with the strong recommendations to listening and accompaniment in the final synthesis."[13]

Yes, I was disappointed that gay people, and all of the marginalised, did not receive a more explicit and emphatic welcome, yet we should rejoice that we are travelling together, even if sometimes with pain and mutual incomprehension. This is a sign of hope not just for the Church but for our fractured humanity.

This synod acknowledged that this does leave a question hanging in the air: How different can the Church be in diverse cultures and yet remain one? "What is considered a violation of a right in one society is an evident and inviolable rule in another; what for some is freedom of conscience is for others simply confusion."[14] Might one have women deacons in some dioceses but not others? There are very few male deacons in Africa. But each bishop has "a duty of care for all the Churches (*sollicitudo omnium Ecclesiarum*)" (Synthesis Report 19 c), and so the Church cannot just be a loose federation of local churches, each going her own way. The Eastern Chris-

13. James Martin, SJ, "The Good (and the Bad) Spirits I Experienced at the Synod," *America*, November 3, 2023, https://www.americamagazine.org/faith/2023/11/03/james-martin-synod-synodality-246425.

14. Pope Francis, "Conclusion of the Synod of Bishops," October 24, 2015, https://www.vatican.va/content/francesco/en/speeches/2015/october/documents/papa-francesco_20151024_sinodo-conclusione-lavori.html.

tian Churches show the Latin Church that already we
are more diverse than most of us realised.

A Time of Pregnancy

In October 2024, the synod will gather again. This is a
long pregnancy, the time it takes for a horse to bear a
foal! As I wrote in my last meditation for the assembly,
this is the time for the seed sown in this session to germinate and begin to bear fruit in our hearts and minds.
"Unity ferments silently within the Holy Church of God"
(Synthesis Report Introduction). Every Christian should
nurture the tender plant of synodality with care, speaking words that encourage and give hope and do not hurt,
which reach out to others with whom we disagree. It is
a time to practice synodal listening and discernment in
our parishes, our dioceses, our religious communities,
our schools and university faculties.

This first session began a process of what Christoph
Theobald, SJ, calls, in the subtitle of his latest book,
"pacification."[15] But the creativity to which he also re-
ferred requires theologians to help the Church to reflect
fruitfully on the many questions we raised. Indeed, the

15. Christoph Theobald, *Un nouveau concile qui ne dit pas son nom?
Le synode sur la synodalité, voie de pacification et de créativité* (Paris:
Salvator, 2023).

word *reflect* occurs twenty-one times in the Synthesis Report. We need theologians to help us listen to the word of God and to understand the living tradition of which we are the heirs and protagonists. In the end, we cannot avoid arguments—not argumentation that is dismissive of other views but that through which we search for a more spacious truth, as in the medieval tradition of the *disputatio,* which we learnt to practice as young friars.

I was surprised, though, by a certain fear of theology. One synodal member told me she thought that the final synthesis was "too theological." When I asked what this meant, she replied, "Abstract." I understand what she means. Academics, too, are tempted by a sort of "clericalism," ways of thinking and writing that are opaque, as if they are the guardians of a secret gnosis, out of the reach of the merely baptised. In Britain, *theological* can mean "irrelevant," as when politicians dismiss a question as "merely theological." But our theology is of the Word of God who became flesh and blood and spoke in parables that still astonish!

We do need brothers and sisters with specialised skills, who can decipher ancient manuscripts and plunge into obscure questions of logic. One of my admirable brethren has devoted his life to interpreting ancient Sumerian tablets. Without exegetes and archaeologists, experts in patristics, philology, and philosophy, logicians and historians, we will drift into using the word of God as ammunition for our agenda, instead of learning "the obedience of faith" (Rom 1:5). We need theologians, men and women, whose ascetical vocation requires hours of solitary labour in libraries at the service of truth.

But this exigent academic enterprise should be at the service of a theology that is truly synodal, born of the conversation between of the word of God and our lived experience. St. John's Gospel is a succession of conversations between Jesus and his friends and opponents through which we are drawn ever more deeply into the mystery of divine love. All of the more technical skills of theology are at the service of truthful and fruitful conversation: faithful to our experience, to life, to the Gospel, and to the tradition. It is surely no coincidence that days after the end of this first part of the synod, Pope Francis issued a document arguing that theology "cannot but take place in a culture of dialogue and encounter between different traditions and knowledge, between different Christian confessions and different religions, openly confronting all, believers and non-believers."[16]

I learnt this the hard way. My first job as a priest was to be a university chaplain in London. I was excited by

16. Pope Francis, Motu proprio *Ad theologiam promovendam*, November 1, 2023, https://www.vatican.va/content/francesco/it/motu_proprio /documents/20231101-motu-proprio-ad-theologiam-promovendam .html.

the prospect. I had studied theology and philosophy for years. I had sat at the feet of inspiring preachers and learned teachers. I had so much to share. Surely the students would love my theology. They would love me! This did not happen. No one came to my theological study groups, and my homilies fell flat. I felt like a failure. But all crises are potentially fertile. In a last attempt to understand why things were not going well, I invited some of the students of the university's Catholic Society to the pub. St. Dominic founded the order in a pub, and so it seemed like a good place for a final attempt to relaunch my preaching. I learnt that evening that, first of all, I must listen to the students to whom I intended to preach, learn from them, and then perhaps, with the grace of God, I might have something to say. Fifty years later, they remain among my closest friends.

For this time before the next session of the synod to be fertile, we need theologians who help us dialogue with others, crossing cultural and political boundaries. We need their assistance in our conversations with the word of God and the tradition. We are in conversation with our ancestors, too, since we are the community of the risen Lord, who has triumphed over death. Then we shall be at the service of that unity in God that spans all time and space, and of the Christ whose resurrection we celebrate when we light the paschal candle, saying:

Christ yesterday and today
the Beginning and the End
the Alpha
and the Omega
All time belongs to him
and all the ages
To him be glory and power
through every age and for ever. Amen.
(The Solemn Beginning of the Easter Vigil or
Lucernarium)

Accountability and Co-responsibility in the Government of the Church

The Example of the Dominicans

Recent crises in the life of the Roman Catholic Church, especially that of the sexual abuse of minors, have made the question of accountability and co-responsibility of the utmost urgency. The words of St. Paul ring in our ears with a new insistence: "[T]he night is far gone, the day is near. Let us then lay aside the works of darkness and put on the armor of light" (Rom 13:12). In a society in which democracy is on the retreat and political power often evades accountability, the Church should embody openness and mutual transparency. I have been asked to explore whether the government of a religious order, in this case the Dominicans, has any lessons to offer the Church in this time of self-questioning.

But how can the government of a relatively small group of men, all trained in theology and philosophy and committed by lifelong vows, be in any way illuminating for the government of a diocese, a complex hierarchical structure embracing hundreds of thousands of people with varying degrees of formation and commitment, and *a fortiori* for the universal Church?

1. Fraternity

Every religious order and congregation is animated by a spirituality. St. Francis, *il poverello* of Assisi, has attracted people in every century by his dramatic imitation of Christ; St. Ignatius of Loyola gave the Jesuits the Spiritual Exercises, the heart of their life and mission; the mystical teachings of St. Teresa of Avila and St. John of the Cross lie at the roots of Carmelite religious life. In contrast, St. Dominic left his brothers and sisters a spirituality embodied in a form of communitarian government.[1]

The brethren make their profession to God and to the master of the order by vowing obedience on the Book

1. "Regimen nostrum suo modo communitarium est." Constitutio Fundamentalis, *Liber Constitutionum et Ordinationum Fratrum Ordinis Praedicatorum* (Rome: Curia Generalitia, 2010).

of the Constitutions and Ordinations of the Order of Preachers. This orders our common life and mission, our fraternity and our preaching. A theological vision of what it means to be preaching friars is incarnated in legislation on government, how chapters are to be held, how superiors are to be elected, how decisions are to be made, and so on. A spirituality embodied in a dry book, mostly concerned of legislation, may seem uninspiring, even legalistic, but it forms the brethren, and the sisters analogously, to live in mutual charity and missionary outreach.

So the first lesson of the Dominican tradition is that a spiritual and a theological vision may be embodied, implicitly or explicitly, in the processes of government, in how decisions are made, how people are chosen for leadership, and how debates are conducted so that everyone's voice is heard. What theological vision do the present structures of church government embody? What vision of the Holy Spirit working in our hearts and minds is incarnate in the decision-making processes? What new structures of government does the Church need if we are to respond to Pope Francis's invitation to embark on the synodal path, a way of government that is "so ancient and so new"? The Dominican tradition suggests that unless a new vision of the Church is embedded in fresh institutional structures, it will remain an unrealisable aspiration, mere words.

Secondly, this Dominican form of government embodies a spirituality that speaks with beauty and clarity to this new moment in the life of the Church. In *Fratelli Tutti*, Pope Francis invites the Church to rediscover its fundamental identity as a community of brothers and sisters. This fraternity, for want of a more inclusive term, is fundamental to the mission of the Church, the gathering of humanity into Christ's kinship. Francis quotes Pope Benedict: "The Church . . . works 'for the advancement of humanity and universal fraternity.' "[2] *Brother* and *sister* are the most ancient and fundamental Christian titles, pointing to the promised unity of all people in Christ.

The title of the encyclical, *Fratelli Tutti*, is a quotation from St. Francis of Assisi, who believed that we are not only brothers and sisters of the extended human family but of the whole of creation, of Brother Sun and Sister Moon and so on. The spirituality of St. Francis's contemporary, St. Dominic, was also fundamentally fraternal. They both founded orders of friars, *fratres*, brothers, and there were Dominican sisters even before there were brethren. Our founder wished to be known only as "Brother Dominic." Fittingly, his first biography is found in the *Vitae Fratrum*, "The Lives of the Brethren," written some thirty years after his death. Rather than a

2. Pope Francis, Encyclical letter *Fratelli Tutti*, October 3, 2020, n. 276; quoting Pope Benedict XVI, Encyclical letter *Caritas in Veritate*, June 29, 2009, n. 11.

towering founder figure, he was one of the brethren. His self-effacement, typical of the preacher who does not wish to get in the way of the Word, is his most beautiful gift to his brothers and sisters.

The way of life of these *fratres* spoke powerfully to the world of Dominic and Francis, in which the old feudal hierarchies were weakening. Democracy was in the air. Strangers, often merchants like Francis's father, were appearing in the new cities. New ideas were being explored in the universities being founded all over Europe and to which Dominic sent his young brethren to study and teach. For this evolving society, a new spirituality was needed to articulate and embody exciting aspirations towards a wider community. Marie-Dominique Chenu, OP (1899–1995), wrote that "every time the word 'brother' or 'sister' resurfaces in the Church, it has a utopian charge, the promise of a world in which strangers will be embraced."[3] Our society is living in an even more intense time of transformation. Pope Francis challenges the Church to reach out to our unknown brothers and sisters in our global village. The spirituality of the friars surely has something to offer a world in which daily interaction with strangers from all over the planet is for some a joy but for others a threat.

3. Marie-Dominique Chenu, OP, "L'Ordre de St Dominique: A-t-il encore sa chance?" Unpublished conference given in Toulouse, October 11, 1970.

2. Friendship

From the beginning, fraternity in the Dominican life predisposed the brethren and sisters to friendship. St. Dominic was known for his affectionate relationship with women, especially young women! The second master of the order, Blessed Jordan of Saxony (1190–1237), wrote letters filled with love to a Dominican nun, Blessed Diane d'Andalou (1201–1236). St. Catherine of Siena (1347–1380) was surrounded by a group of friends, the *Caterinati*, whose mutual affection and teasing overflows from their correspondence, and she had an especial fondness for Blessed Raymond of Capua, OP (1303–1399), afterwards master of the order. After the Fall, it is hard to think of any easy friendships in the Bible between men and women until the coming of Christ. A sign of the breaking-in of the kingdom was the band of disciples, men and women, who accompanied Jesus in his mission. It was, above all, the women who stayed at the foot of the cross and who were the first witnesses to his resurrection. The joyful friendship between these early Dominican brothers and sisters can be an inspiration for our society, in which the relationships between woman and men are often fraught and fearful, and a sign of the coming of the kingdom.

The tendency of this fraternity to overflow into friendship finds its theological underpinning in the trinitarian theology of St. Thomas Aquinas (1225–1274). For those early Dominicans, friendship was more than mutual affection; it was a sharing in the eternal, equal friendship that is the very life of God. Only God's grace can overthrow the inequality of God and creature to embrace us in friendship. As Aquinas put it in the *Summa Theologiae*, "*Solus Deus deificat*"—only God can make us godlike.[4] Pope Francis summons us beyond the stifling clericalism that has deformed so much of the Church's life for centuries. The Dominican model of fraternity predisposed to friendship offers hints as to how this may be lived.

This vision of fraternity also helps us better to understand the nature of the scandal of sexual abuse and its cover-up. Brothers and sisters are called to live together in the clear light of the truth. More than illicit sexual relationships or the exploitation of power, though sexual abuse is both of these, it is the betrayal of friendship, our participation in the friendship of God. At the frozen heart of Dante's *Inferno*, Satan devours three figures whose treachery betrayed friendship. The Church can only transcend the crisis of sexual abuse, seeking forgiveness for its failures and offering forgiveness for those who committed the abuse, if we are able to attain a certain clarity about the nature of the betrayal, which has caused such pain and scandal. How can friendship be reknit after such a betrayal?

4. *Summa Theologica* I-II, q. 112, a. 1.

3. Truth and Unity

The fraternal spirituality of the Order of Preachers is embodied in our communitarian form of government. This has enabled the Order to live fruitfully the irradicable tension between two necessary constituents of brotherhood, especially as it matures into friendship: truth and unity. *Veritas*, the motto of the order, is not merely a matter of factual accuracy, much as that matters. More than requiring just a dispassionate examination of facts, it is our shared search for the truth which Christ has promised will set us free (see John 8:32). Yves Congar, OP (1904–1995), famously said, "I have loved the truth as I have loved a person."[5] This passion for truth, which has imbued the best of Dominican life for eight hundred years, should ideally carry us beyond divisions in our search for the One who is the Truth and who transcends all our conceptions and ideologies. St. Albert the Great (1200–1280), Aquinas's master, claimed that the greatest delight lies in "seeking the truth together, in the pleasure of companionship" (*in dulcedine societatis quarere veritatem*).[6]

But Dominican life has always been, and always will be, marked by tensions between different understandings of the Gospel and the teachings of the Church. When our

5. Quoted in Colleen Mary Mallon, OP, *Building Bridges: Dominicans Doing Theology Together* (Dublin: Dominican Publications, 2005), 97.

6. *Politica*, Bk. 8, vi, in *Opera Omnia*, vol. VIII (Paris: 1891), 804.

brother Gustavo Gutiérrez, OP (b. 1928), the founder of liberation theology, was summoned by the Congregation for the Doctrine of the Faith, he encountered brethren who perhaps were not so committed to his radical option for the poor! The order embraces every part of the theological spectrum and has sometimes been on the verge of fragmentation. During the divided papacy of the fourteenth century, St. Vincent Ferrer (1350–1419) championed a different candidate for the papacy than St. Catherine of Siena and the brethren who were her friends. When the Church was swept by an enthusiasm for strict observance, led in the order by friars such St. Antonius of Florence (1389–1459), Fra Angelico (1395–1455), and Girolame Savonarola (1452–1498), the unity of the order was threatened, as it was again by the rise of nationalism at the beginning of the nineteenth century. But the order hung on to its unity by the skin of its teeth. This was not because of any superiority to other orders that have been fruitfully fissiparous but because our vocation as preachers of the kingdom, in which all will be one in Christ, would be betrayed if we resigned ourselves to division.

As the Church today embarks on the synodal path, the tension between truth and unity is felt acutely everywhere. Many fear it will lead to schism. The Church in Germany is watched with hope by some and dread by others, as is the plenary assembly of the Church in Australia. If the Church openly debates its life and mission and gives voice to many contending positions, how will it hold together? This has been the challenge for the government of the Dominican Order from the beginning, which is why it might be worth studying for the lessons that it could yield for the Church as a whole.

Sara Parvis of Edinburgh University observed, in a document prepared for the Bishops Conference of Scotland in light of the 2021–2024 Synod on Synodality, that "the word 'synod' offers us a paradox: it means 'a way taken together,' implying a dynamic movement, but it generally refers to a static moment when the Church, or a portion of it, stopped and asked each other for directions, because it wasn't clear which way followed Christ, the one who is the Way. The newly-coined term 'synodality' attempts to solve this paradox: it puts forward as a necessary habit of the Church the constant readiness to ask one another for directions, with differing degrees of formality and in different organisational contexts, if the way becomes unclear."[7]

Dominican government embodies one way, tried and tested over eight hundred years, of listening to each other as we seek the way forward. Our government is capitular

7. Sara Parvis, "Synodality in Scripture, in Tradition and in History," unpublished paper. A summary was presented at an online conference organised by the Bishops' Conference of Scotland, *Synodality in the Life and Mission of the Church: A Deep Dive into the Themes of the Synod*, February 12, 2022, https://www.youtube.com/watch?v=JxyUuk9QGCU, minutes 31–32.

and communitarian. Arriving in Rome in 1992 as master of the order, I was immediately summoned by the head of a Vatican dicastery, who was rightly concerned by the provocative actions of the brethren of one of our provinces. I was instructed that "as the supreme authority in the order," I must act immediately. He was puzzled when I explained that I was not the supreme authority. "Who is it then?" he asked. I responded: "The brethren"!

4. "Take Your Time"

Some religious orders seek unity in a shared vision of their common life and mission. In the Dominican tradition, I would suggest that rather than a unity of being "of one heart and soul" (Acts 4:32), it lies in a *process* of government that demands endless time, the exigent discipline of listening to each other in chapters: general, provincial, and conventual. These consume that most precious treasure, time. General chapters are held every three years, with representatives from every province in the order, usually lasting about three and half weeks. They are expensive to host, and the order is not rich. An English Dominican objected to my predecessor as master, Damian Byrne, that general chapters were a waste of time and money. Byrne replied that chapters are like breathing. One may not notice their efficacy, but if one were to stop, one soon would. Without their regular oxygenation of the order's lungs, the order would disintegrate.

There are moments of joy but also weeks of tedious work in commissions, preparing documents that are endlessly discussed, amended or rewritten, and voted upon. During the first chapter in which I participated thirty-three years ago, there were hints of the polarisation that was beginning to afflict the Church. But over successive chapters, this tension has diminished, and we have learnt to listen to each other at length, usually with open hearts and minds.

The process of Dominican government aims to carry us beyond ideological combat but at the cost of much time and patience. Sara Parvis looks at these processes at work in the Acts of the Apostles and St. Gregory Nazianzen (329–390) and the Council of Constantinople of 381. She concludes that the process of reaching agreement was painfully slow: "Our case studies remind us that the fruits of synodality rarely ripen in one generation. Aligning the way forward with tradition across time and space matters too much. Great clashes of culture, theology and ecclesiology and the Church's response to them have to be lived out over at least seventy or eighty years before the Church as a whole is in a position to appreciate what is ephemeral and what is really of the faith."[8] We still witness the Church digesting the conclusions of the Second Vatican Council more than

8. Parvis, "Synodality in Scripture," 12.

fifty years after its closure. Unsurprisingly, the process of assimilation is quicker with a small group such as the Dominicans, but even so Damian Byrne maintained that decisions of general chapters usually took nine years to *begin* to impact the life of the order.

So the second lesson of the order's tradition of government is that the synodal path will demand profound patience and the commitment to a long process of mutual listening. That is the inescapable cost of holding the people of God together in truth and unity. This is countercultural in our society of instant communication, instant judgment, and instant gratification. Our politics are dominated by short term goals, rarely reaching beyond the next election, and businesses often seek short-term profits within the current financial year. But the government of the people of God, nurturing the search for truth and unity, demands a patience that will seem frustrating and even irresponsible to many in our impatient culture.

When, for example, the synod of bishops for the Pan-Amazon region in 2019 did not yield the changes many longed for—such as the ordination of married priests—many people felt betrayed and angry. But the Dominican process of government suggests that the synodal Church needs to enculturate a different understanding of time, organic rather than mechanical. A shortcut to victory by any group would subvert the organic process of good government, leading either to fragmentation or an imposed uniformity. Ludwig Wittgenstein, the Austrian philosopher, said, "This is how philosophers should salute each other: 'Take your time.'"[9]

Revelation took millennia. That we need patience will be incomprehensible to many. For Dominicans, this is sustained by a life of shared prayer that stretches over decades, of friendships that cross theological and political differences. What shared life is needed in the Church if she is to embody God's slow greening and long-awaited springtime? How countercultural can the Church be without succumbing to the isolation of a sect?

5. Conversation of Free Brethren

Dominican government is founded on conversation in chapter, seeking consensus. If consensus is not attained, the radical innovation of the order in the thirteenth century was to take decisions by majority vote. Conversations within chapters are at the service of the preaching, the conversation between the Gospel and the multiple ways in which contemporary human beings make sense of their lives. If we cannot talk with each other, how shall we be able to talk to our world? So the process of

9. Ludwig Wittgenstein, *Culture and Value* (Chicago: University of Chicago Press, 1984), 80.

capitular government is based on the assumption that the shared search for the truth should overcome discord. Debate should not aim for the victory of a party but the ever-fresh discovery of the truth.

Paul Murray, OP, claims that for Aquinas, this passion for the truth should carry us beyond all that is narrow and partisan:

> St Thomas, in a letter sent to a certain Brother John, concerning study, wrote: "Do not heed by *whom* a thing is said, but rather *what* is said you should commit to memory." And, again, in another place: "When taking up or rejecting opinions, a person should not be led by love or hate concerning who said them but rather by the certainty of truth. He [Aristotle] says we should love both kinds of people: those whose opinions we follow, and those whose opinions we reject. For both study to find the truth and, in this way, both give us assistance."[10]

Fundamental to Dominican government and fruitful conversation is trust in the brethren that puts us at ease and free with each other. One cannot control the evolution of a conversation! A German adage in the late

10. Paul Murray, OP, *The New Wine of Dominican Spirituality: A Drink Called Happiness* (London: Burnes and Oates, 2006), 116.

Middle Ages was "*Stadtluft macht frei*"—"City air makes free." In the thirteenth century, a strong wind of freedom was blowing through the new cities. People were freer to travel and to think new thoughts. The order was founded in the same year that the *Magna Carta* was written in England, a declaration of the freedom of the barons from the tyrannical rule by the king. We do not in practice have a rule but constitutions, which are always open to revision. Dominic is pictured with a knife since he said that if the brethren became scrupulous in their obedience to the constitutions, he would cut up every copy. Our way of government forms us for freedom and is founded on Dominic's confidence in his brethren. He did not want our legislation to bind under sin, "since you are no longer slaves under the law, but a people living in freedom under grace."[11] When Dominic sent out his novices to preach, some Cistercians were scandalised at his confidence in the young. He replied, "I know for certain that my young men will go out and come back, will be sent out and will return; but your young men will be kept locked up and will still go out."[12] Church government today needs to embody this bold confidence in the young.

11. Fundamental Constitution VI, quoting the Rule of St. Augustine 7.4.

12. Tugwell, *Early Dominicans*, 91.

6. Beyond the Culture of Control

Our society is shaped by what David Garland has called "the culture of control."[13] Charles Taylor, in his masterpiece, *A Secular Age*,[14] explored the shift at the beginning of modernity from a view of the world as organic, open to the transcendent, to the triumph of a mechanistic perception of reality, in which the dominant metaphor for change is that of the clock! Government was achieved through pulling the levers of power, exercising control.

But for Dominican government, confidence in the brethren implies a certain surrender of control. One cannot control the Spirit. Pope Francis has insisted on this surrender to the unpredictable promptings of Spirit: "There is no greater freedom than that of allowing oneself to be guided by the Holy Spirit, renouncing the attempt to plan and control everything to the last detail, and instead letting him enlighten, guide and direct us, leading us wherever he wills. The Holy Spirit knows well what is needed in every time and place. This is what it means to be mysteriously fruitful!"[15] Pope Francis, therefore, believes that we must not be afraid of a bit of mess.

13. David Garland, *The Culture of Control: Crime and Social Order in Contemporary Society* (Oxford: Oxford University Press, 2002).

14. Charles Taylor, *A Secular Age* (Cambridge, MA: Harvard University Press, 2007).

15. Pope Francis, *Evangelii Gaudium*, n. 280.

He said during the 2013 World Youth Day in Rio de Janeiro, after the downpours of rain: "I expect a messy World Youth Day. But I want things messy and stirred up in the congregations. The Holy Spirit hovered over the chaos in the beginning, and the creation came to be. We should not fear a little confusion, even chaos, if we are to be open to the Spirit's renewal. Such talk is alarming to tidy minded people!"[16]

So church government, having confidence in the faithful who have received the Holy Spirit, should embody a tension, which for some is hard to bear and difficult to negotiate, between the need to make decisions and to steer the Church in a certain direction and yet at the same time a loss of control as we are moved by the "unruly freedom"[17] of God's word. What one person may consider to be an openness to God's unpredictable Spirit another will condemn as the flight from responsibility. Finding that balance is surely one of the daily challenges that Pope Francis faces! It is an art to be discovered rather than a science that can be learnt.

This trust in the brethren also takes the form of a strong insistence on subsidiarity. Masters trust the provincials and provincials trust the priors and local communities to take

16. Impromptu words of Pope Francis on the last day of the World Youth Day, Rio de Janeiro, July 28, 2013.

17. Pope Francis, *Evangelii Gaudium*, n. 22.

the right decisions and should interfere as little as possible. For this reason, unlike other orders, the members of the general council stay away from provincial chapters, so that there should be no hint of any interference from above. When my general council and I arrived in Rome in 1992, the repeated advice from our predecessors was, "Trust the brethren, even if you think that they are mistaken." This led to some amicable disagreements. What if we thought that the decisions of the provincial and his council showed a lack of trust of the brethren of the province?

The purpose of visitations is not to impose decisions from above, but to animate and stimulate the conversations of the fraternity and help dialogue to recommence if it has broken down. They should ensure the co-responsibility of the brethren at every level. So visitations are more about asking questions than imposing solutions: Are the challenges of preaching the Gospel being addressed? Do the brethren have real dialogue with each other? Are any groups or individuals unheard or misunderstood? Are decisions implemented? If there is a breakdown in government, the conclusion of the visitation will usually propose a process to reignite the fraternal dialogue. Government is primarily at the service of conversation.

Surely, one of the roles of the bishop is to animate the conversations of all the members of the Body of Christ under his care. Who is unheard or silenced or ignored? How can dialogue reach across ideological divisions and boundaries so that the pursuit of truth and unity are held together? Are the voices of the young heard? The typically Protestant temptation is to champion truth at the expense of unity. The Catholic weakness often is to insist on unity to the detriment of fearlessly seeking the truth. Both are premature resolutions of a tension that will always and necessarily abide.

7. Diverse Forms of Authority

Let us now consider some of the elements of Dominican government, which should sustain our conversations when they are most difficult. Every friar has received the Holy Spirit and so speaks with authority, even when we believe his view to be wrong. There must surely be some grain of truth to be welcomed, even if ultimately one does not accept his position. The International Theological Commission published a document on the *sensus fidei*, the personal understanding of the faith of every baptised person. It quotes the first letter of St. John: "[Y]ou have been anointed by the Holy One, and all of you have knowledge. . . . [T]he anointing that you received from him [Christ] abides in you, and so you do not need anyone to teach you" (1 John 2:20, 27).[18] If the vote in chapter

18. International Theological Commission, Sensus Fidei *in the Life of the Church*, n. 1.

goes against the convictions of a group of brethren, they must know that not only have they been heard and honoured, but that their position is somehow registered by the chapter in its final decisions.

The unity of the chapter is sustained by our intense shared life for several weeks. Decision-making takes place within the context of hours of praying together, listening to each other preach and share our faith, eating and recreating together. The chapter is a profound experience of living fraternity, which often gives rise to unexpected friendships that cross ideological divisions. One becomes attuned to the hopes and fears of the capitulars, not only to what they say but how they use particular words, the aesthetics of their discourse, their struggle to find the right expression.

This fraternity embraces everyone present at the chapter—the guests invited from the other branches of the Dominican family, the Dominican friars and sisters who are translators, interpreters, secretaries, photocopiers, drivers, cooks and those who serve at table. The whole experience of the chapter should be of brothers and sisters living together in equality, bound together by shared prayer, debate, and recreation. These different modalities of communion are woven together. Decision-making in the dioceses needs also to be rooted in the *humus* of the common life, prayer, and relaxation of the whole people of God.

Parvis points out that the earliest readers of Acts would have been aware that all those involved in the debates that shook the early Church—especially Peter, James the brother of the Lord, and Paul—were eventually called to martyrdom, "giving their lives for Christ, however divided they were in their ecclesiology."[19] Each of them, therefore, had authority as a witness to the Gospel for which they shed their blood. As individual dioceses and the whole Church embark on the path of synodality, every member of the Body of Christ must be recognised as having his or her authority as a baptised Christian who has received the Holy Spirit. More fundamentally than proponents of a party line, we are all are fellow disciples, seeking to know God's will.

In the chapters of the order, this means that every capitular has the same right to speak and to vote. During the debates of the chapter, the master of the order intervenes as little as possible and usually only to clarify issues, rarely to champion a position. He is there to listen and subsequently implement the decisions of the chapter. Yet we do not all speak with the same kind of authority on every subject. It quickly becomes evident with what sort of authority a brother speaks, whether as a theologian, a missionary, a pastor, an administrator, or a bursar.

19. Parvis, "Synodality in Scripture," 3.

If I were to speak about finance, everyone would soon realise that it is not with the authority of an expert!

If you will forgive a brief diversion: As dioceses and the Church embark on the uncertain and unpredictable synodal path, the recognition of the authority of every baptised Christian is fundamental. However, especially when there are tensions over complex issues, different sorts of authority are in play. St. John Henry Newman believed that in the Church there were three authorities, or offices.[20] There is the authority of "devotion," of the experience of God, which is shared by the whole people of God. We all have authority because of our baptism, confirmation, and encounter with the Lord in prayer. There is also the authority of truth sought by reason. This is an especial responsibility of trained thinkers, above all theologians. The Church needs people who wrestle with difficult issues, pose hard questions, and doggedly go on questioning even when this alarms some. Finally, there is the authority of government. This is especially invested in the hierarchy of the Church. Newman maintained that no single form of authority must predominate. We may propose a different analysis of the types of authority involved in the debates of our time—the early Church

20. John Henry Newman, Preface to the 3rd edition of *Lectures on the Prophetical Office of the Church* (London: 1874) and the 3rd edition of the *Via Media* (London: 1877).

insisted on the authority of martyrs, and today we are exhorted to listen to the poor—but it is surely true that we all have authority but differently, which is why complex doctrinal issues cannot be resolved by a simple vote, as Pope Francis insisted after the Amazonian synod.

Clarification as to how authority in all its diverse forms interacts is vital if the synodal path is to avoid either fragmenting the Church or disappointing those who are eager for change. Here, perhaps, there could be a fruitful dialogue between the Dominican tradition of communitarian government and the Jesuit tradition of discernment, to which Pope Francis is so deeply indebted.

In Dominican government, this recognition of different forms of authority finds a partial expression in membership of consecutive general chapters, held every three years. After a general chapter to elect the master of the order, there is a chapter of elected diffinitors. These capitulars cannot be provincials. These chapters often show the bold creativity of those who are not directly responsible for implementing the decisions of the chapter! Three years later there is a chapter predominantly of provincials, who are likely to be more focused on what is considered practical by those in leadership. Different constituencies each have their moment of authority. Then there is another elective general chapter, consisting of both provincials and diffinitors. All new legislation is only incorporated into the Book of Constitutions after being ratified by all three forms of chapter with their diverse memberships. A sequence of chapters with different sorts of capitulars goes back to the origin of the order.

8. Imagination

Conversations that reach across ideological divisions require the imagination to understand why people sincerely hold views with which we disagree. Fergus Kerr, OP, asserted during a chapter of my province in 1996,

> If you ask me to say what I prize more and more the longer I am in the Order . . . then I have to say that it is a way of thinking—of expecting other people to have views we may disagree with; expecting also to be able to understand why they believe what they do—if only we have the imagination, the courage, the faith in the ultimate power of the truth, the charity to listen to what others say, to listen especially for what they are afraid of when they seem reluctant to accept what we want them to see.[21]

So dialogue leading to decision-making demands not just rational debate by imaginative sympathy and

21. Acts of the Chapter of the English Province of the Order of Preachers, 1996.

a charitable hermeneutic that is attuned to what others are trying to say, even if inarticulately and misleadingly. We should be gentle midwives to each other's insights, especially when we are uneasy with the ideas that are seeking articulation!

There was a heated debate on preaching at the general chapter of 2013, held in Krakow, over the nature of preaching, always a hot topic for us! The document proposed to the chapter by a commission understood preaching in dialogical terms: we proclaim our faith by entering into conversation with people of other faiths or none. Some capitulars strongly disagreed, arguing that this verged on relativism. We must dare to preach the truth that we have received boldly. Slowly it became evident that the brethren were speaking out of very different experiences. The principal author of the commission document had spent his Dominican life in Pakistan, where Christianity necessarily finds itself in constant dialogue with Islam. For more than four decades, the Federation of Asian Bishops' Conferences has insisted on the threefold dialogue—with the poor, between cultures, and with other religions—which is at the heart of the Church's mission.

The brethren who reacted strongly against the document were mainly from the former Soviet Union. For them, the idea of a dialogue with those who had imprisoned or tortured them made no sense. A way forward could not be found solely through rational argument, though that had its part to play. An imaginative engagement with the experience of the other was necessary. This demanded a *process* of mutual listening, as so often in our form of government, during and after the chapter. We had imaginatively to enter the lived experience of brethren who were unable to accept what we considered to be evident.

9. Accountability

A third requirement of good government is accountability. The master submits a report to every general chapter, three in the course of his mandate, his *Relatio de Statu Ordinis*. This a substantial document. My last *Relatio* was over twenty thousand words long, giving an account of the state of the order, its strengths, weaknesses, and challenges. This is examined by the chapter and forms the starting point of many of its debates. For example, in 2010, the master's *Relatio* presented the case for a radical simplification of the different levels of government of order, which the chapter discussed, accepted, and began to implement over subsequent chapters. The provincial, too, must render an account of his government to the provincial chapter.

Financial transparency is a touchstone of accountability. One of the first crises in the life of the Church was over the distribution of funds in Acts 6, which led to the naming of the first deacons. Parvis again: "The phrase *diakonein trapezeis*, which describes the new ministry, is often translated as 'serving tables,' but since *trapeza* is the normal word for a bank, it may in the context mean 'serve as bankers,' i.e. as administrators or bursars, holders of the community funds and disbursers of them for the good of the poor, here specifically the Greek-speaking widows."[22]

At every general chapter, the syndic of the order must present the central accounts of the order and propose a budget for the chapter's approval. The master and his council have control of only very limited resources. The headquarters of the order, at Santa Sabina in Rome, is financed by a tax on the provinces, in accordance with each's income. A sensitive issue at every chapter is whether every province is completely transparent about its financial state so that an equitable budget can be proposed and approved. Financial transparency is a litmus test of our mutual trust, without which our government would be impossible.

Unsurprisingly, the toughest nut for Pope Francis to crack is the reform of Vatican finance. Trust, as we embark on the synodal path, demands complete financial

22. Parvis, "Synodality in Scripture," 6.

transparency at diocesan and parochial level, though in places of persecution, this may not be possible.

10. Elections

Fundamental to Dominican government is the election of superiors at all levels: the master, the provincials, and the priors. The election of priors is approved by the provincial and of provincials by the master. There were attempts by the Vatican during my mandate to impose approval of the election of the master by the Pope, as is the case with some other religious orders, but this was vigorously and successfully resisted. In the early Church, there was some form of election of bishops by the diocese. The forms taken were diverse and the results often deeply divisive, fuelled by party politics.

Has the Dominican experience of election anything to offer the Church today? Every election is preceded by a *tractatus*, an extended discussion by the capitulars of "candidates," an appropriate term for a Dominican election, since its original meaning was someone who wore white! For the election of the master, the process extends over five days. In my experience, the discussions are always honest and charitable. They are a deeply moving expression of our fraternity. To talk about one's brethren in a way that both protects their good name and honestly gauges their suitability for office is a sacred trust. It is a most intense expression of our fraternity, seeking the truth while cherishing unity. One of the few times that I intervened as master in the election of a provincial was when it was evident that the *tractatus* had not been well conducted. The due process of debate had not been respected, and so I required that it begin again, not so that another candidate be elected but so that the election might be the fruit of truly fraternal conversation.

Might we envisage some such process in the choice of bishops, even if we do not return to direct elections? The present pope of the Coptic Orthodox Church, Theodore II, was chosen in 2012 at the end of a process in which local assemblies of clergy, lay men, and lay women— involving 2,400 people in all—put forward names that were whittled down to a short list of three. These were put in a chalice on the high altar and a blindfolded boy picked out one to be the new pope. Omitting that final stage surely, might not we imagine a similar process of extended consultation within each diocese so that the people of God are heard as they were in early centuries? It would demand a formation in the profound responsibility that goes with speaking charitably about people's fitness for office. Again, this is countercultural in our society, which brims over with accusation and denigration. We must discover how the Church can sustain another culture without retreating into a narrow sectarian identity. Or, how can the Church be inculturated in the diverse cultures of our world without succumbing to all that is divisive in them?

In the Order of Preachers, all offices are held for a limited mandate, only repeatable once. Until the end of eighteenth century, the master of the order was elected for life. Now his mandate is for nine years, and in practice (except in a state of emergency, such the First World War), he is never reelected. No brother should become cemented in a position of responsibility, especially bursars! Ordination to the episcopacy and presbyterate is sacramental, and so presumably cannot be just for a limited time. The bishop is wedded to his diocese, even if this sometimes takes the form of serial monogamy. How, if at all, should the principle of limited mandates apply to positions of diocesan leadership?

11. Institutional Creativity

A last question of maximum importance but to which the experience of Dominican government can only give a minimal input: How is the voice of the laity, and especially of women, to be heard in the Church?

Even before the foundation of the Order of Preachers, St. Dominic gathered communities of brothers and sisters, who were contemplative and active, religious and lay. Yet the unity of what came to be known as "the Dominican family" did not lie in unified government.

Although the master presides over the Dominican family, each branch in different ways and degrees fiercely guards its own juridical independence, especially the active sisters. We are guests at each other's chapters, with voice but no vote. So does the Dominican experience offer any wisdom on this most urgent question? We found that institutional creativity is needed. This the Church has shown endlessly throughout its history.

Let me give just one example. At the last count, there were 167 congregations of active Dominican sisters, with about thirty thousand members in total. Each congregation cherishes its own juridical independence. In 1995, a new organisation, Dominican Sisters International (DSI), was established so that without compromising the independence of each congregation, Dominican sisters could establish new forms of collaboration with each other and with other branches of the Dominican family. DSI has its own council, which, at least when I was master, met twice a year with the general council of the friars. For the first time in eight hundred years, there was a formal structure for collaboration in equality between the brothers and sisters.

We need institutional creativity within the Church if new voices are to be heard and granted authority. Despite the popular impression, the Church has never been a monolithic hierarchical structure but a complex web of different institutions witnessing to different experiences and giving voice and authority to different members of the Body of Christ. What new institutions might we need if lay women and men are to be heard today in the Church's debates?

Conclusion

In conclusion, the essential challenge of Dominican government in all the areas we have considered remains that of holding truth and unity together, always in fruitful tension. I have argued that this necessitates a patient listening, often extending over years. It demands that we have imagination, trust, and transparent accountability, especially about finance! This can only be sustained by a way of life that is countercultural. It is difficult for members of a religious order to sustain this way of life, which so goes against the grain of contemporary culture. How much greater is the challenge for a diocese or the Church to be both of our time and in touch with the people of this generation, and yet embodying a culture in which loving conversation between all is possible!

Selected Bibliography

XVI General Assembly of the Synod of Bishops. *Instrumentum Laboris for the First Session (October 2023).* https://www.synod.va/content/dam/synod/common/phases/universal-stage/il/ENG_INSTRUMENTUM-LABORIS.pdf.

XVI General Assembly of the Synod of Bishops. *Synthesis Report, First Session (4–29 October 2023).* https://www.synod.va/content/dam/synod/assembly/synthesis/english/2023.10.28-ENG-Synthesis-Report.pdf.

Acts of the Chapter of the English Province of the Order of Preachers, 1996.

Aelred of Rievaulx. *Spiritual Friendship.* Notre Dame, IN: Ave Maria Press, 2008.

Alison, James. *Knowing Jesus.* Springfield, IL: Templegate, 1993.

Azpiroz Costa, Fr. Carlos A., OP. "'Let Us Walk in Joy and Think of Our Savior': Some Views on Dominican Itinerancy." May 24, 2003. http://dominicains.ca/lettres-des-maitres-de-lordre/?lang=en.

Benedict XVI, Pope. "Meeting with the Parish Priests and the Clergy of Rome: Address of Pope Benedict XVI." February

14, 2013. https://www.vatican.va/content/benedict-xvi /en/speeches/2013/february/documents/hf_ben-xvi_spe _20130214_clero-roma.html.

Benotti, Riccardo. *Viaggio nella vita Religiosa: interviste e in- contri.* Vatican City: Libreria Editrice Vaticana, 2016.

Bergoglio, Jorge Mario, and Abraham Skorka. *On Heaven and Earth.* New York: Image, 2010, 2013.

Betto, Frei; aka Carlos Christo. *Letters from a Prisoner of Con- science.* London: Lutterworth, 1978.

Carretto, Carlo. *I Sought and I Found: My Experience of God and of the Church.* Translated by Robert Barr. Maryknoll, NY: Orbis, 1984.

Castellano, Giovanni, OP. "Was This Synod a Waste of Time?" Dominican Dispatches substack, November 5, 2023.

Cavallini, Giuliana. *St. Martin De Porres: Apostle of Charity.* St. Louis, MO: B. Herder, 1963.

Chenu, Marie-Dominique, OP. "L'Ordre de St Dominique: A-t-il encore sa chance?" Unpublished conference given in Toulouse, October 11, 1970.

Chesterton, G. K. *Orthodoxy.* London: Hodder and Stough- ton, 1996.

Constitutio Fundamentalis. *Liber Constitutionum et Ordi- nationum Fratrum Ordinis Praedicatorum.* Rome: Curia Generalitia, 2010.

Conway, Placid, OP. *Saint Thomas Aquinas: A Biographical Study of the Angelic Doctor.* London: Longmans, Green, 1911.

Eagleton, Terry. "What's Your Story?" *London Review of Books*, February 16, 2023. https://www.lrb.co.uk/the-paper/v45 /n04/terry-eagleton/what-s-your-story.

Ernst, Cornelius, OP. *The Theology of Grace*. Theology Today Series, vol. 17. Dublin: Fides, 1974.

Faggioli, Massimo. "Notes on Prophecy and the Ecclesiology of Synodality from the Second Vatican Council to Today." *Irish Theological Quarterly* 88, no. 4 (November 2023): 308–22.

Francis, Pope. Apostolic Exhortation *C'est La Confiance*. October 15, 2023. https://www.vatican.va/content/francesco /en/apost_exhortations/documents/20231015-santateresa -delbambinogesu.html.

Francis, Pope. Apostolic Exhortation *Evangelii Gaudium*. November 24, 2013. https://www.vatican.va/content /francesco/en/apost_exhortations/documents/papa -francesco_esortazione-ap_20131124_evangelii-gaudium .html.

Francis, Pope. "Conclusion of the Synod of Bishops." October 24, 2015. https://www.vatican.va/content/francesco /en/speeches/2015/october/documents/papa-francesco _20151024_sinodo-conclusione-lavori.html.

Francis, Pope. Encyclical letter *Fratelli Tutti*. October 3, 2020. https://www.vatican.va/content/francesco/en/encyclicals /documents/papa-francesco_20201003_enciclica-fratelli -tutti.html.

Francis, Pope. "Intervention of the Holy Father at the 18th General Congregation of the 16th Ordinary General Assembly of the Synod of Bishops." October 25, 2023. Holy See Press Office. https://press.vatican.va/content/salastampa /en/bollettino/pubblico/2023/10/25/231025f.html.

Francis, Pope. "Meeting with Young People of Scholas Occurrentes, Greeting of His Holiness." Apostolic Journey of His

Holiness Pope Francis to Portugal on the Occasion of the XXXVII World Youth Day, August 3, 2023. https://www.vatican.va/content/francesco/en/speeches/2023/august/documents/20230803-portogallo-scholas-occurrentes.html.

Francis, Pope. "Message of His Holiness Pope Francis for the 57th World Day of Social Communications." January 24, 2023. https://www.vatican.va/content/francesco/en/messages/communications/documents/20230124-messaggio-comunicazioni-sociali.html.

Francis, Pope. Motu proprio *Ad theologiam promovendam*. November 1, 2023. https://www.vatican.va/content/francesco/it/motu_proprio/documents/20231101-motu-proprio-ad-theologiam-promovendam.html.

General Secretariat of the Synod. *"Enlarge the Space of Your Tent" (Is 54:2)*. Working Document for the Continental Stage. Vatican City. October 2022. https://www.synod.va/content/dam/synod/common/phases/continental-stage/dcs/Documento-Tappa-Continentale-EN.pdf.

Hillesum, Etty. *An Interrupted Life: The Diaries and Letters of Etty Hillesum 1941–43*. London: Persephone Books, 2007.

Hollerich, Cardinal Jean-Claude, SJ. "Speech by His Eminence Cardinal Jean-Claude Hollerich, SJ." October 4, 2023. Holy See Press Office. https://press.vatican.va/content/salastampa/en/bollettino/pubblico/2023/10/04/231004e.html.

International Theological Commission. Sensus Fidei *in the Life of the Church*. Vatican, 2014. https://www.vatican

.va/roman_curia/congregations/cfaith/cti_documents
/rc_cti_20140610_sensus-fidei_en.html.

Ivereigh, Austin. "How the Synod Will Change the Church."
The Tablet, November 11, 2023.

Lamb, Christopher. "The Church Begins to Dream." *The Tablet*, November 4, 2023.

Levi, Primo. *Survival in Auschwitz*. New York: Touchstone, 1996.

Lewis, C. S. *The Four Loves*. New York: Harcourt, 1988.

Mallon, Colleen Mary, OP. *Building Bridges: Dominicans Doing Theology Together*. Dublin: Dominican Publications, 2005.

Martin, James, SJ. "The Good (and the Bad) Spirits I Experienced at the Synod." *America*, November 3, 2023. https://www.americamagazine.org/faith/2023/11/03/james-martin-synod-synodality-246425.

Martin, James, SJ. "What Happened at the Synod on Synodality." *America*, October 30, 2023. https://www.americamagazine.org/faith/2023/10/30/synod-synodality-james-martin-246399.

McCabe, Herbert, OP. *God Matters*. London: Darton, Longman and Todd, 1987.

McEnroy, Carmel. *Guests in Their Own House: The Women of Vatican II*. New York: Crossroad, 2011.

Merton, Thomas. *Conjectures of a Guilty Bystander*. New York: Doubleday/Image, 1989.

Merton, Thomas. *The Seven Storey Mountain: An Autobiography of Faith*. Fiftieth Anniversary Edition. Orlando: Harcourt, 1998.

Murphy-O'Connor, Cormac. *An English Spring: Memoirs*. London: Bloomsbury, 2015.

Murray, Paul, OP. *The New Wine of Dominican Spirituality: A Drink Called Happiness*. London: Burnes and Oates, 2006.

Murray, Paul, OP. *Scars: Essays, Poems and Meditations on Affliction*. London: Bloomsbury, 2014.

Newman, John Henry. Preface to the 3rd edition of *Lectures on the Prophetical Office of the Church*. London: 1874.

Paris, Leonardo. *L'erede: Una cristologia*. Breschia: Queriniana, 2021.

Parvis, Sara. "Synodality in Scripture, in Tradition and in History." Unpublished paper. Video presentation of summary at https://www.youtube.com/watch?v=JxyUuk9QGCU.

Pérennès, Jean Jacques, OP. Foreword by Timothy Radcliffe, OP. *A Life Poured Out: Pierre Claverie of Algeria*. Maryknoll, NY: Orbis, 2007.

Pétrement, Simone. *La vita di Simone Weil*. Milan: Adelphi, 2010.

Pongratz-Lippitt, Christa. "Pro-reform German Bishops Warn against Going Too Fast." *The Tablet*, March 20, 2023. https://www.thetablet.co.uk/news/16829/pro-reform-german-bishops-warn-against-going-too-fast.

Radcliffe, Timothy. "Accountability and Co-Responsibility in the Government of the Church: The Example of the Dominicans." *Studia Canonica* 56, no. 2 (2022): 587–604.

Radcliffe, Timothy, and Łukasz Popko. *Questioning God*. London: Bloomsbury, 2023.

Rahner, Hugo, SJ. *Man at Play, or Did You Ever Practice Eutrapelia?* Translated by Brian Battershaw and Edward Quinn. London: Compass Books, 1965.

Reese, Thomas J. "What Pope Francis Forgot about the Media: You Either Feed the Beast or the Beast Eats You." *America*, October 20, 2023. https://www.americamagazine.org /faith/2023/10/20/synod-synodality-media-246340.

Sacks, Jonathan. "Elijah and the Still, Small Voice." rabbisacks .org/covenant-conversation/pinchas/elijah-and-the-still -small-voice.

Second Vatican Council. Dogmatic Constitution on Divine Revelation *Dei Verbum*. In Austin Flannery, ed., *Vatican Council II: Constitutions, Decrees, Declarations*. Collegeville, MN: Liturgical Press, 1996, 2014.

Second Vatican Council. Pastoral Constitution on the Church in the Modern World *Gaudium et Spes*. In Austin Flannery, ed., *Vatican Council II: Constitutions, Decrees, Declarations*. Collegeville, MN: Liturgical Press, 1996, 2014.

Taylor, Charles. *A Secular Age*. Cambridge, MA: Harvard University Press, 2007.

Theobald, Christoph. *Un nouveau concile qui ne dit pas son nom? Le synode sur la synodalité, voie de pacification et de créativité*. Paris: Salvator, 2023.

Thérèse of the Child Jesus and the Holy Face, Saint. *Letters II: 1890–1897*. Washington, DC: ICS Publications, 1988.

Tugwell, Simon, OP. *Early Dominicans: Selected Writings*. Mahwah, NJ: Paulist Press, 1982.

Weil, Simone. *Waiting on God*. Translated by Emma Crauford. London: Routledge & Kegan Paul, 1959.

Wright, Cathy, LSJ. *Saint Charles de Foucauld: His Life and Spirituality*. Boston: Pauline Books, 2022.

Wright, Scott. *Oscar Romero and the Communion of the Saints*. New York: Orbis, 2009.